Letters to Kirabelle

BY BECKY CLIFFORD

DORRANCE
PUBLISHING CO
EST. 1920
PITTSBURGH, PENNSYLVANIA 15238

Dorrance Publishing Co
585 Alpha Drive
Pittsburgh, PA 15238

Visit our website at *www.dorrancebookstore.com*

ISBN: 978-1-6853-7292-7
eISBN: 978-1-6853-7828-8

Letters to Kirabelle

Acknowledgments

A special thank you to my husband Stan who has been not only my rock but my safe space, my partner, my copilot on this life adventure, and someone who knows me on a very deeply beautifully profound level. To Kira – you inspire me in so many ways and I have learned so much from being blessed to be your Mom. To my pups – you are the bestest teachers of unconditional love and I am thankful for the snuggles, licks, Halloween costume photos, and walks outside. To my heavenly angel – I am thankful to have a little navigator up there and I love you so stinkin' much. To the female mentors in my life starting with my amazing mom, my aunts, and my grandmother – you all inspire me in different ways and I honor your strength, your stories, your courage, your tears, and your unique beauty. To my two brothers Mike and Pete and my sister Monica – the three of you I have looked up to in different ways for many years and am thankful to have you in my life. To my dad – thank you for enjoying my soccer games, VA Tech visits, and Ingerick Family Reunions. I couldn't have asked for a better dad. To all of my extended family and friends – my roots are thankful to be connected to yours.

To Gabbie Berstein's writing group of strangers that finally got this book to its completion by knowing that my dream was shared by many and that we all could do it.

To all of the people that I met along my journey so far and were able to share hope and pure human exchange, I honor you and remember you. All of the love and real moments have left imprints on my heart and amazing memories.

May our paths to true acceptance and love unite us all as we journey forward.

Foreword

Dear Mom, I love you so much. You get me and our time together means a lot. You make me laugh. You are kind and the best thing about you is you are you. The thing is you worked so hard to make a book for me and I know it's hard and sometimes you just don't know what to write, but you are SO creative. I am proud of you.

Love,
Kira

This book is a memoir about my journey through cancer to then having my daughter Kira two years later and then moving from the U.S. to Switzerland to live in the land of cheese and chocolate to then returning "home" to the U.S. to continue my life journey. The idea is for it to be snip-its of things I would want my daughter to know about me (truly madly deeply), my journey, and the resiliency of the human spirit as well as the divine power of LOVE.

Table of Contents

Chapter One

ARE YOU THERE, BECKY? IT'S ME...CANCER

Side note: Do you remember Judy Blume?
Loved her! I mean who didn't love stories about Fudge?

...MY EYES OPENED AND I SAW THE NURSE AND MY HUSBAND STAN. A little bleary-eyed from the anesthesia given with a colonoscopy... I was quite aware that this meant the procedure was complete and I could now go home and that I could EAT something! Hallelujah! I had no idea the news I was about to get. This round of recent doctor's visits started a few months prior because I had blood when I pooed and I was quite positive that it was hemorrhoids or something embarrassing for a thirty-one-year-old to have but definitely nothing serious, nothing life threatening...right?! I had my entire life ahead of me to live. I had recently gotten married and moved from Virginia to New Jersey, and started a new job and really was ready for the next logical step in my imaginary probably watched too many movies life which in my eyes was to have babies... however Stan wanted to wait another couple years. He wanted to enjoy "couple" time as he called it. We were realizing in marriage, that we were not always going to align on everything and this was becoming more and more clear to us. He wanted to buy a house, I wanted to buy baby clothes. He wanted the blue house, I wanted the yellow one we saw. My maternal instincts were callin' ....or was it something else calling?

The blood was only little bits at first, intermittently and I let it go on for a while. I did some WebMD googling of my own and determined the worst it could be was IBS or hemorrhoids. Then when I was at my friend Michelle's wedding (I was a bridesmaid) I remember the following day so much blood came out of me I honestly thought it was my period until I checked where it was coming from as I was pretty hungover. I called my OBGYN in a bit of a frenzy as she had just put me on thyroid medication and I asked her if the meds could cause some stomach bleeding as some of the warnings say on drug medication commercials and she said "no" and then quickly ended the call. Dude, my butt is bleeding lady. Huhlow? I then visited my general doc who said it's probably nothing after she did a physical exam and couldn't find anything but just to be sure, she gave me a script to go get a colonoscopy. I had no idea what a colonoscopy was or that it involved shoving a tube up my butt and exposing my rear end to a bunch of strangers. Lovely. Just lovely. But the sight of that much blood was not something I could ignore. So I made the appointment, completed the horrid prep, and showed up.

And when I woke up post-procedure, I remember the nurse saying that the colonoscopy was over, the procedure went okay, and that the doc was going to come speak with me. There was an element of me that was proud of having just undergone something that involved a horrid prep the night before and then a tube being stuck up my bum. That was intense and scary. And now it was over. Enter long exhale. I also felt a bit thinner kind of like back in the day when I overused laxatives or made myself throw up. Eating, self-image, body image – they had been an issue for quite some time. The doc came and sat at the foot of the bed and the words that came out of his mouth next sent a bolt of traumatic shock and utter disbelief through every part of me. Stan even went blurry for a while – who knows what he felt or thought in that moment. The doctor said, "I found a large mass. I am pretty positive it is cancer."

As I faded in and out of my ability to hear clearly or even know my name, he went on to explain the mass was being sent to the lab for further testing and that I would definitely have to have surgery but that maybe that was it. He was calm and professional in his delivery but also heartfelt and caring. He was present with me in my fear and he was prepared to sit at the side of my bed until I was ready to get up or at least that's how it seemed to me. I kept asking questions like if he had seen this before in someone my age? For whatever reason, I wanted to know I wasn't alone. I mean when I first came in for the procedure the lady who asked me some pre-procedure questions even found it odd that my non-overweight, under thirty-five, non sleep apnea otherwise healthy looking individual was scheduled for a colonoscopy and my doc who ordered it even got yelled at for it not making protocol sense, yet I am very thankful she did. The doctor said he had indeed seen it once in a young girl and the mass turned out to be cancerous and she had surgery and was fine after that. This ONE case gave me HOPE. I mean surgery wasn't something that excited me but the fact that I could get "it" taken out, my colon reattached, and still be able to use the john and move on with my life was a pill I could swallow. The one where I had nasty treatments, lost my hair, became frail and died wasn't one I wanted to partake in. I was scared at what it all meant but I managed to keep my eye on the ONE story, the one that gave me hope, and put one foot in front of the other. I got myself up, dressed and left the hospital room determined to hang on to hope and keep repeating that one story about the girl who lived.

Later that week, we went Christmas shopping at the mall because we were going to Virginia in about three weeks where my family lived and where I grew up and I needed to get some gifts. I remember my phone ringing in American Eagle and I grabbed it immediately when I saw an unfamiliar number. Side note: I have to thank cancer for coinciding with my favorite time of year – Christmas. At least I found out my majorly shitty news during Santa's busiest time of spreading joy and peace.

I picked up the call and was told that the first lab results that came in said it was inconclusive. Wait, so you tested it and you aren't really sure? Are cancer cells drastically different or just a tad? Or was the pathologist having a tough day? Why can't you know? In this moment, I had to become comfortable with the unknown and with this particular answer that I had at this particular time, which obviously was a tad different than the answer I wanted and had envisioned which was "sorry big mistake! You are fine!" Or the one where my alarm clock goes off, I wake up and these past few months were ALL a vivid scary dream.

The voice on the other end continued to tell me that it appeared precancerous but there was no way to be certain until it was removed and retested. After some talk with my parents and Stan's parents about where to have the surgery – Stan's dad suggested Memorial Sloan Kettering in NYC because when it came to cancer – they were the "best of the best". At the time we lived in Easton, Pennsylvania so NYC was a doable car ride or bus ride away. And I loved the big city also known as the Big Apple. I always felt alive when I went there. Granted also over stimulated and at times quite anxious but alive. There was so much going on, so much hustle and bustle, so many different cultures being blended together in one spot with lights and cameras and action, and the empire state building...okay now I sound like the unbreakable Kimmy Schmidt who was let out of the bunker but hey – I stayed in Virginia a really long time.

The doctor who did the colonoscopy also recommended a surgeon in Pennsylvania. We decided to meet with both doctors and make a decision after. I remember going into the city and seeing our first choice. It was big. It was nicely decorated and everyone seemed to be really nice, friendly, and knowledgeable. They wanted to see the mass for themselves so they did this slightly different procedure where I laid under a sheet with a room full of people and a screen. Together, we saw the mass. I only remember parts of this because I don't know, when someone has a tube shoved up my bum, it was hard for me to get past that detail and to remain present, completely present. I remember trying to focus, breathe, pray and wish it over. Parts of me still held on to that same thread of hope that this was all just a scary dream. How had my life changed so quickly? This was so not part of my logical next step. They took some samples, and later their lab results showed that it was indeed cancerous but the doc reminded me that it was possible that all I needed was surgery.

Wait what?! So I did have cancer? I don't know about you but my entire life the word cancer was never associated with any good story that didn't involve death. My two grandparents, my friend's mom, etc. Wasn't cancer a death sentence? Didn't it mean having horrible medicine that made you puke and lose your hair and not want to eat and then you eventually pass and people mourn your loss? I was TOO young. Even though I spent a LARGE portion of my adolescent life hating my body and a lot of time wishing I was thinner or prettier – I wasn't ready to leave this earth. Parts of my life were fun, especially when I was drinking and could suppress all the voices that told me I wasn't good enough and that saw this often times distorted image of myself. What I didn't know then that I know now is that I think cancer came into my life to wake me up to a much deeper healing, a much deeper relationship within that I needed to look at. And fast forward to today – ten-plus years later – I am thankful for this life changing awakening. As hard as it was – I see more clearly now than before. I am thankful for the chance I got to fight and to move forward and it totally changed my outlook on illness, healing, serving, and living.

Prior to this appointment, I had Googled the chances that the procedure of taking out the sigmoid colon where the mass resided and reattaching my bowels could go wrong and I read all about the possibility of having a colostomy bag. I even tried to work through well at least if that happens, I AM ALIVE in my head. Would Stan still love me? What would sex be like? Would people treat me differently? These were all the questions running through my head but no matter what the predicament, this one thing was clear…. living some more was better than DYING. I think in contemplating this one thing – I found more gratitude in what all I did have and it gave me a different feeling inside. I think it is part of human nature in working through stuff, accepting that with life – comes suffering and that when you truly look at your life – you can find something to be grateful for. It can be something really small yet the healing power of gratitude can be quite large. And I was grateful no matter what to be alive, to be able to get medical care, and to have a fighting chance.

So when we discussed with the surgeon, I couldn't help myself but to ask about the chances of the colostomy bag based on my readings and I remember him saying less than 1 percent would need a colostomy bag and I was like, "Well, it was less than 3 percent that someone my age would get this to begin with," and he said, "Well then, consider your bad luck already over."

I remember this sentence sending a wave through me and I thought to myself – hey good way to spin that. Back to all that I did have. A 99 percent chance of no colostomy bag and a good bit of hope. He was confident and he had beautiful dreamy blue eyes that were like looking into a crystal clear lake on a sunny day. That is what I remember about the surgeon himself. Some people have these eyes that you can't help but stare into which was even more awkward for me because in the back of my head I also knew this man saw my ass along with several other strangers of a growing list. The more times I had procedures that involved shoving things up my rear or talking about bowel movements, the more this acclimated to being "normal" and my neighbor then got me a book *Everybody Poops* which helped me laugh about my situation and normalize that we all do have butts and we can talk about them. And…that your digestion and poop are very telling to your overall health!

So fairly early on in this cancer crisis, I learned two things. One – HEALTH IS A PRIORITY and my body is a gift and I would never again take it for granted and I would try to keep my vessel clean. Two – Each small moment became so much more cherished and I therefore became and felt so much more alive and happy in the midst of this storm. For years prior – I worried about all this other trivial stuff for so long – not being liked, not being thin enough, and yet I failed to thank my body for the millions of processes it goes through every day to keep me walking, talking, and breathing not to mention the countless friends and good family I had. I was also surprising myself in my adaptation and processing of the news as it came and forging ahead. I was proving to myself that I was stronger than what I had thought and maybe what others had thought based on my small, thin, at times socially awkward, soft spoken feminine frame. Who said small and shy means weak? Didn't we all love *Rudy* the movie? Didn't

Mother Teresa make an impact on the world? Who is to judge some-one else's inner strength based on appearance and who am I to be such a critical judge of self? But we all can accidentally try to box people up, beat ourselves up, filter us or them into groups, and draw lines in our sandboxes. I was showing up for myself and with each big step I took – gaining confidence I could do this. I was becoming that little red engine that thought she could and would beat cancer.

We left the doctor's office not comforted by the fact that it was in-deed the big "C" but by the fact that we liked the place, trusted the doctor, and we both felt at peace with the decision.

A couple weeks later we met with the other doctor, the one the co-lonoscopy doctor recommended whose office was in an old house in Bethlehem, Pennsylvania. It had a totally different vibe and this par-ticular doctor had only done a few of these surgeries so I didn't feel quite as keen on going with this one so we decided to go with the one in NYC. I will never know the what ifs…I am sure he could have done a fine job but at the time I had to follow my gut – literally and figura-tively. And for me maybe I was drawn to the fun side of NYC. When one is handed lemons, was I making my own lemonade? I mean shoot, why not squeeze the juice out of life since I was learning nothing was guaranteed and that my life was so very precious.

I had an appointment for pre-op testing so I came in to have blood work done which involved another trip to NYC so Stan and I made the day of it. We took off work and planned to explore the city afterwards, have a nice lunch, and try to make it fun. Stan and I are both very hard-working people and quite hard on ourselves at times with quite high expectations. When he is at work – he barely takes bathroom breaks and sometimes I wonder if he breathes deep. I was also very fast at what I did, I loved the analytical piece and if someone asked me to do some-thing – I did it. I didn't play the "busy" card and I wasn't interested in politics or politicking myself – if that is a verb. To some people in the corporate world – this was my downfall. In my mind it was simple, I was there to do a job and I did it and I tried to do it well and to see things from different sides. So for us both to have a day off and turn some focus towards getting me better whilst having fun kind of bonded us. When your life or health are at risk, life has a way of bringing one back to the present moment and today we had a day off work and some fun NYC vibes. This is what I thought, I have no idea what it was like to be Stan….he seemed to handle it all pretty darn well and was able to be my rock and for that I was also uber thankful.

I remember being really nervous and wishing it was over so we could get to the "F.U.N" part of the day. I think the nurse could tell that I was wrapped up in my own thoughts because she started to randomly tell me a story. And I remember thinking that I wished she would just be quiet and get the testing over with – I didn't feel like talking…
..But as she told the story, I started to listen more and more. She grabbed me out of my internal self-talk and into the present moment – the here and now so that we could connect. It was like she pulled me out of this dark corridor into one with natural lighting. She told me she was left in her country to die of an illness but that she miraculously got better and now lives in the U.S. and is a nurse. Her brother however she told me, healthy as a whip one day was shot in NYC running through Central Park and died. He lost his family and his children in basically the blink of an eye. I am not sure that I even responded or if I just looked at her but I remember thinking months later that that one woman told me in that one moment exactly what I needed to hear. She didn't have this large "look at me" presence but she administered something so large and so powerful. She gave me yet another dose of perspective, hope, and a reminder that life isn't guaranteed to any of us. That even though I may have been told I had cancer and had to face

surgery – the rest of my life was still unwritten. To this day, I am thankful to her and those other people I began to meet along the way that fed the hope and didn't add to the fear. They left crumbs on my path. They left marks on my heart. They left beauty in my life. I am forever thankful. Cancer is not always an easily accepted social thing....because for lots of people it brings up bad memories, fear, trauma, loss. It can be a trigger. But those that put their lives up to a greater being, that heal their wounds and remain present, those that hold true to miracles, and those that can be that source of strength for those that aren't, without judgement, are remarkable and more of what I now strive to be. Those that can help someone step back from staring at just one tree to see the entire forest and the much larger lake of possibility and hope. And to those that can stay present with someone as they are, in one moment connecting fully.

The good news of the day was that my heart was fine. No problems there. Operation could commence and NYC day of fun was about to begin.

Stan and I then went for lunch and enjoyed the Big Apple. To us, we knew that we had to get through the surgery but we had trust that we were in good hands, support from our family, friends, faith, and hope that after the operation – that would be it for me and I could go back to my "normal" life. Or would it ever be normal again? Would I then transfer into a "new normal"? Reading this line now during a pandemic – I can relate to this idea of "normal" changing and that being okay. I can also relate from a mother's perspective because your entire previous normal is no longer. It is this idea of resurrecting or reconstructing yourself again and again and again that can be really beautiful. Albeit, hard.

I was nervous leading up to surgery but both working and it being the start of the holiday season (my most favorite time of year as possibly mentioned before) definitely helped. My parents planned to come to the city and we had a hotel room for the night before. I felt comforted to know that the three strongest links to me were going to be there, my mom and dad that brought me into this world and loved me unconditionally and my husband who took vows to promise to be by my side in sickness and in health (ironically I was a bit tipsy when I took my vows to deal with being in front of peeps) and well this was the pinnacle of sickness we could have ever imagined. And it was now our reality. Through it all, he was my pillar of strength and I only wish now to stay strong and to be able to be that for him, and for you Kirabelles when you need it. As days went by, I continued to amaze myself, and be amazed by those around me with the power of the human spirit, one's will, and one's ability to love life, love each other, and to heal. And what I have also learned and sort of questioned afterwards is how the fear of cancer has come to be and how it has spread. It seems to get marketed as "deadly" and I wonder if this could change?? I mean "silent killer" to me seems kinda harsh. What exactly is it that makes the topic often taboo? Is it the way the disease is portrayed or personal experience of loss or the "business" around it? I don't know. But around some words – fear builds. Well for me, having made it to the other side and having met some survivors who can attest to this – it changed my life and me for the better and I don't feel sick, I feel more alive now and after than I felt before. In many ways, it was one of my many teachers. One of our many teachers? A wake-up call. A nudge. A much needed deeper awakening. Cancer isn't as prevalent in all parts of the world.....So much can come from crisis and I think we are all learning that now in the midst of a pandemic. A collective mother freakin' wake-up call?

I remember later having a massage lady in Jim Thorpe, Pennsylvania who let me in on a little secret – that she herself was a breast cancer survivor....she said that when you survive it is almost as if you enter this secret club. A club of people who can't help but ooze gratitude for their life, who see beauty in the spirit, who feel the breeze and coolness of the air with a sensation that hits their inner soul, we love deeper, we feel deeper, and sometimes this allows us to soar higher. It also comes with a weight. The fear when you feel something inside like a cold or a tingle that it could be something more, that it could be a recurrence, that you could face it again. But at this point, I could only hang on to the hope of joining that secret club – my journey had just begun. And her story, again gave me hope, perspective, and connection and I was thankful that she shared.

I remember having to do yet another colon cleanse prep before surgery so it was hard to truly enjoy the city with all that was about to occur, but we sure did try. My mom, God bless her, has a knack for the chit-chat, and listening to it totally got me out of my head. I have no idea what she said to me for about twelve hours but my brain really tried to divert from myself and my inner turmoil and listen to it. When people say the "gift of gab" – it is one of her strengths and she rocks at it. She and my dad were able to remain loving, calm, and cool and were there for me. My dad was more restless and had to get up and leave the room at times, etc., but he was there. He showed up. The morning of surgery I was definitely nervous, anxious, and I remember that story of footprints in the sand – God was definitely carrying me that day. Prayers, thoughts, well wishes, and love were carrying me that day. I do remember the anesthesia guy talking about the drug he was about to shoot in my back and referring to it as some really good tequila and this did get me laughing and remembering my college times dancing with hot dudes or on top of a bar. (Daddy may not let you read this part until you are forty-five.) Once I was under the in-fluence of this said really good tequila, my memories turn a little cloudier. I remember being entered into the operating room. I remember how I was laid on a sparkly shiny silver table that was super COLD. And then I was out.....

Hours later, I remember waking up. It was dark. I remember the nurse telling me right away the surgery was over, that I had been given something for pain and as it wore off I needed to tell her right away so they could get the pain under control. I remember upon waking feeling as if I was healed, as if something bad and heavy and dark was now removed from me and I had this vision that my grandmother had told me in my dreams while I was asleep, she had come to me and told me that I was going to be okay. Later I told my mom this but I think the drip of morphine I was getting made her laugh it off or maybe she herself felt it too but didn't want to stay in that place remembering the loss of her beautiful amazing mom while her daughter lay in a hospital bed. Maybe she couldn't go there with me. I remember my mom, dad, and Stan being brought in to see me as I awoke in the recovery room. Man, to see them in that moment – the thought still brings me to tears. It is so easy to get caught up in life sometimes that we forget – how much loved ones mean to us and how precious this time is. Life may seem long at times but really – it's pretty short. Our time here on earth is precious. Earth is precious. Our physical beings are precious.

They were ushered out and waited patiently until I was moved to what would be my room for the next approximately five to seven days. What I hadn't even thought about until later on.... Was their side.

Dealing with this on their side. I was drugged. In a way, I had it easy. I didn't have a way to feel pain, worry, fear. I felt numb and sorta flying high. I had just completed the hard part (or so I thought) and it was time to recover. What about them? They loved me and they didn't have anything other than their faith that I was going to make it to the other side and a lot of waiting. I remember Stan saying the surgeon came out earlier than expected after surgery and when he first saw him – he was so scared that he was going to hear bad news. But instead the surgeon told them it was over, I was well, and they would get to see me soon. The tuuu-mer (it's kinda fun if you say it like Arnold) we'll call it enemy #1 had been sent away for further testing and I had signed some pre-surgery paperwork to donate the tumor to research along with the paperwork I signed giving all my possessions over to someone else in case I died. It's a shame you sign this one before the really good tequila!

Chapter Two

LOVE HEALS

I GOT MOVED INTO MY ROOM WHICH I STAYED IN FOR ABOUT A WEEK. I was given this contraption to breathe into to help strengthen my abs and I was also given a pillow to apply pressure as I tried to get up from the bed. Which I DO REMEMBER the first time getting up – man the Pain with a capital P. Woah Nelly. But I did it. The nurses were incredibly nice. After a few days I remember one of them helping me wash my hair. The way she brushed my hair is something I will never forget. Again, it evokes tears in me sometimes to think about the many angels that were put along my path of recovery. It may sound silly to some to say she touched me by washing my hair but I think it was the love and care that emanated from her as she did it. There are people that do their job and people that DO their JOB, and as humans we probably have a bit of both. No one is immune to bad days or times. In that moment, she whole-heartedly gave of herself and her time to help a sister out, as my hair was starting to get that greasy hair clumped together look. I want to go back and hug each and every one of the amazing nurses, staff and doctors that stayed present with me, that treated me with love and kindness. They aided in my healing. I want all those courageous nurses that daily attend a job that nurtures people in need, people who are sick, people who need help, to know how in awe I am of them. I want them to know as a survivor afterwards how much I wanted to pass it along and truly love those around me and be with them. It made me think of jobs as not a means to a paycheck but a much larger way to serve. It was no longer about stability or how much money that job could bring me, it was more of the reach I could have on others and how true deep healing has a large impact on society and those around you. There are such lessons from the tragedies and tribulations of life if we can reframe them as they are occurring. If we can remove labels and welcome them in as our best teaching moments that may have an opportunity to unite rather than divide. #together we rise# During times of tragedy and I learned this more through my yoga studies – blame and shame can be easy to turn to but they are not part of the divine. They do not help yet instead further us from our healing and create more armor.

I also made friends with another patient on the floor. We were encouraged to walk or take laps to get our circulation going so I did mine in the morning often around the same time as another recoveree. She had had her entire stomach removed – also from cancer. She was a beautiful lady. We would walk and chat and laugh. Life kinda slowed down when I got sick and within the slowing – each moment had a lot more zest and life. I think the staff even took notice of the fact that we walked together each morning. I also remember running into one man that was just getting up and I had been walking for days and he joked with me that I made it look easy. And I joked back that by the end of the week he would be doing laps with us. And in that moment when we exchanged those words and our eyes met, all I could feel was his smile back, and his fighting spirit and in my head, I prayed for us both – that we both would make it. That we both would see better days.

So things were progressing and that is when Stan and I got a visit from the white coats. I say white coats because that is all I remember about them walking into my room. I remember these starch white clean coats and I remember the look on their faces not being one of rejoicing but one that didn't really want to show any emotion – sort of just blank but serious, very serious and businesslike; kind of like the people on *24* in the interrogation rooms. Okay – so maybe I am exaggerating a hair, but who doesn't like television and this is how it felt to me. It was then they confirmed that the tumor was indeed cancer. They had removed thirty-one of my lymph nodes and found a tiny microscopic piece in three of them. Due to this recent find, they recommended what they called adjuvant chemotherapy to make certain that they got all of it. At the time I knew nothing about adjuvant therapy or stages or that stage 3 was scarier but I did have ideas about what chemo was like – hair loss, puking…and none of that appealed to me. It was a pretty hard blow and I remember it being somewhat out of body again. Like I was there physically but I went off to another place as they were talking. Me??!! Chemo??!! I was just on the verge of believing I was over this hump and well, the hump or hill just got a bit wider, vaster, bigger, and scarier.

This is when things got a little tough. It hit me hard. There was a lot of crying between Stan and me. I had a lot of questions about what this meant in terms of survival, of my hair, of what chemo did to my chances of ever being a mom? And we were met with some tough answers. The protocol for this type and stage was six months of chemo followed by scans every six months for the first two years and then it would move out to once a year. Within the first two years of the diagnosis, I had a 25 percent chance that it would return and I would die within five years. Now, being a financial analyst who is good at numbers, 25 percent is something I like to hear for a clothing sale but not when it comes to a chance at dying. One in four?! But there was another number involved – a 75 percent chance of living was better than a 25 percent chance of dying – check. I also reminded myself if I was to go, that I had lived an incredibly fun thirty-one years. I had tons of friends, tons of memories, a husband, an adorable puppy, a house, a job. Life wasn't so bad. I had lived long enough to graduate high school, college, learn to drive, go on some awesome spring breaks, have a wedding, and a lot of good times were had. I remember asking the surgeon on my own one morning as he tended to make his rounds around 3 A.M. about the possibility of my having children. His bed side demeanor that morning – ehhh…wasn't what I wanted to hear. He said, "If you live, then you can try." It wasn't like he said anything wrong or mean but I remembered feeling flat in that moment. Feeling afraid. Feeling like he knocked down every ounce of inspiration and hope and comfort that maybe I was searching for. He tested my faith and maybe just maybe made me dig a little deeper and believe in me despite what anyone else said in the matter. This was my life and I couldn't give up on my dreams. Being a mom was one thing in life that was super clear that I wanted to experience. I had dreams when I was young of being a teacher or a fashion designer and a few other things but I always felt inside I was going to have a baby, I was going to be a mom. I remember telling my mom that even if I never got married, I was going to adopt a girl so I could braid her hair and take her shopping. I had plans in life. I had goals. I had dreams.

The other piece of good news was that I probably wouldn't lose all my hair. The particular kind of chemo they were recommending was 5 FU and Oxaliplatin and while they came with a long list of side effects including thinning hair, the docs informed me most people didn't lose all of their hair with colon cancer treatment. They repeated that a few times. This was incredible news for a blond young woman who was already self-conscious about her appearance. And when I was intoxicated,

I actually liked my hair and thought on some nights I looked quite cute.

Another thing I remember about my hospital stay was this class on make-up that was given for free that I attended. This is where I thought this particular hospital was pretty smart with everything. It was me and about four or five other female cancer patients in a room being taught some make-up tips. We were learning and engaging our brains in how to feel good about ourselves and pamper ourselves on the outside, regardless of the war that may be going on inside of us. To proudly show our faces amongst the crowds that would whisper or think "she might die" or "what happened to her hair?" Cancer is a funny disease socially as I stated before. I am guessing all disease is or can be. Because it can carry shame and blame. And I am not sure how much of that is on the patient and the crowd around them…and one thing that we all have in common – dying and sometimes with that the fear of dying. Maybe somedays we can handle it better than others and vice versa. Cancer did change my life forever. Some people live with a fear of it. I met it, know it, and am okay with it. It does sometimes, as my therapist says, step into my tent again in the form of oh, not what if? And my therapist encourages me to invite it in like all of the fears I hold. They have shown up again to teach me something. And if I sit with the fear and I chose to face it– it does not stay long.

Some people fear those that have had it or do have it. Some people I think even think you must have done something to get it. And this sure as hell doesn't make it any easier to survive. But like I said before, Cancer changed me and in many ways for the positive – the journey taught me so much. It can (I hope and pray for those facing it today) help you see the beauty in you, in life, in hope, and in struggle. It can awaken you to some real simple amazing moments and the body's miraculous ability to heal. And how LOVE does heal. It's like a big huge dose of the best medicine. Those energetic moments where we let our guards down and see each other and feel each other – and transmit and transmute love – those are where it's at. Those are Godly moments. The stuff I would like to box up sometimes for the tough days but I must remind you that that well of love and joy Kirabelle – is always inside you. You came into this world so connected to it. Life will sometimes make you want to cover it or go up into your head and "power through" things but the real true power is this well. It can always be tapped into.

I remember the day I got to go home. Stan was beyond excited. We had had some visitors the week I was in the hospital. Two of my college friends who lived in the city at the time came to see me. We had shared a few laughs. I think the morphine drip made me funnier. One night I told the nurse who I remember looked like Donald Faison "Murray" from *Clueless* – I told him they were like the ghost busters. They cleaned house and then sent people home saying, "I ain't afraid of no ghosts." I also remember a lot of discussion about Cheetos and the orange film they leave on one's fingies as they finish off a bag.

Stan does not like going to doctors and hospitals and he wanted to have this part over with so my going home was a HUGE step and a major win. The chemo was to start January and I was to have a port put in, but for the rest of December I had time to recover and celebrate Christmas (enter chorus – my most favorite holiday!) with my family. So again, it wasn't exactly what we had hoped for but it wasn't what we feared the most either. It was something smack dab in the middle – teaching us boat loads as we maneuvered our way through it. Together. Your dad was so loving through all of it. His love never wavered.

This time I had not working was kind of fun. I had always worked. I started working in high school at TJ Maxx with my friend Michelle. And on college breaks, I would work two jobs – one at a clothing store and I tried my hand at being a waitress. Gosh I was a horrible waitress.

There was one time I served a drink not realizing part of the machine had fallen off and into it and another time I made a chocolate milk with so much Hershey's syrup in it that the next time I came around, the boy's head was laying on the table and he had a stomach ache.

So not working at all was kind of a nice break. I still knew I had a job – I just had an entire month off and I didn't know anyone at the time who could or would take an entire month off? I didn't necessarily love my job but I did grow to love the people and the family that work creates, and my illness bonded us. We went through it together. I still have the group card they sent to the hospital that on the front has a hospital gown fashion show with all different sorts of gowns being represented on a runway. It made me chuckle then and it still makes me smile now.

While on this break, I loved being able to watch *The Ellen DeGeneres Show*. When she would start the show with a dance on the coffee table, often days I would join her. Being able to move without pain and to pee and poop were all things I no longer took for granted. This may sound silly but there isn't a poop that goes by where I am not grateful my shoot still works after being reattached and proud at how regular and healthy they look! In those moments, watching Ellen, I could move and I could be silly and I was alive and I felt it more so than EVER before. I would shake my booty on the dance floor like no other after a long island iced tea in college but this time…THIS TIME…. I was doing it completely sober and completely in the flow and I felt SO alive, so grateful and so in love with my life. I didn't expect that this cancer thing would teach me so incredibly much as I lived it.

I also tried to find productive ways to occupy my time. I learned to latch hook. Now Stan may argue after seeing my creations whether this was productive or a waste of cash flow. I mean who doesn't need a furry cat pillow or five? I bought one of those kits at Michaels and man did

BECKY CLIFFORD

I like the action of it. There was something about doing something with my hands that was so repetitive and also had that sense of completion and challenge that was quite therapeutic. The problem was my finished product was, I admit, hideous and I never knew what anyone did with these latch hooked items. To this day I am not sure what I did with the finished product but I remember the creating and completing of it. My neighbor friends came over and cooked for me one night. That was fun. I remember the love and joy of having friends here for me even if I now only had part of a colon and talked about poop a good bit more than before. They accepted me for me and that was all that mattered to me.

The other thing I did a ton of was READING. I read every book that was recommended to me about holistic approaches to fighting cancer. It was hard for me to sit back and just let the doctors do their work. I had to do something and I was curious. I wish I had kept a list of all the books I read. A few ones I definitely recommend are Kris Carr's *Crazy Sexy Cancer*, Lance Armstrong's *It's Not About the Bike*, and Bernie Siegel's *Love Medicine and Miracles*. Ironically my bro sent me Lance's book and my sister Mo sent me the Siegel one. Kris Carr – I found on my own. I read about diet, supplements, and stories of people like Lance Armstrong that survived the bleakest of percentages and lived to tell. I read about survival. I read about taking care of oneself. And I enjoyed a lot of what I read. A lot of it made TOTAL sense. A lot of it gave me hope. A lot of it gave me strategy and a lot of it gave me the tools to heal on a much deeper level. And I enjoyed reading and learning. The better I ate, the better I felt. I also started doing yoga and I fell in love with this type of movement and practice. I remember leaving class feeling like everything was going to be okay. I felt healthy. I felt alive. I felt energetic. I felt love. The more I moved my body – the more I learned about the specific energetic energy channels, ayurvedic medicine, and how to better support my body. And it all made again, – a whole lot of sense! The more yoga I did – the better I felt both on and off the mat. I learned a lot of breath techniques that have helped me and continue to help me today. Connecting to the breath connects one to the moment, to what they are feeling and right now the world is energetically messy and chaotic so it is quite easy to get disconnected. My yoga practice and self-study allowed me to stand tall on my own two feet and honor my patterning and work to create space for me to feel and to heal and to come back to love and acceptance again and again and again. I don't think yoga is a hippie dippie cop-out on life – I think it is a way to feel shiz to the fullest and not self-medicate or tune out or press on. I love it and that is why I later wanted to teach yoga. I had no idea how much I would learn as I started to teach it – but that is for later!

Anyways, your mom gets a little sidetracked when she tells her stories sometimes. That year – we traveled to Virginia for Christmas with my family. My nephew wasn't that old and it was good to see him and to hold him and just be with my family. Again, holiday time is my most favorite time of the year….. I know I know I said this already. Growing up, I have fond memories of all four of us kids in the minivan with my parents and presents next to us driving seven hours to upstate New York to spend Christmas at my grandmother's house. We would spend countless hours in her basement playing pool with the cousins and watching MTV music videos. My mom would make incredible amounts of the most delicious Christmas cookies and we would get so many presents. After my grandmother passed away and we got older, it was now held at my mom's house every year and it was still so special, so joyous, and something I looked forward to. Being with family, having time off of work, and celebrating in the spirit of Christmas. This year was even more special because I was so connected to the moment and to gratitude. I was so alive in spite of all that had just happened physically.

I think for a while I went through life with a very physical attachment to the earth and a need to achieve and listen and work hard but something inside was a bit dead, a bit mute, a bit dark. It's like I couldn't let go and be free and see all of my unique gifts – instead I always felt like there was something to change, fix, or improve. My practice of yoga and mindfulness was really allowing me to see beauty not only in myself but also in very simple parts of my life and the outside world. I remember the exact spot I sat on the couch as we unwrapped gifts. And I remember coming to my brother's gift to me. Everyone in my family knows when it is my eldest brother Mike's gift because of his distinct handwriting and squiggle under his name on the card. My brother growing up was an interesting fellow. He is very smart, kind of quiet, an intellectual, a witty sense of humor, an amazing drawer – like in my opinion could work for *Peanuts* and also quite frugal. Before meeting his wife, he lived in a teenie tiny place and ate peanut butter sandwiches, worked and read books in his free time. I am not even sure if not using jelly on the PB sandwiches was a taste decision or a cost-cutting measure, I will have to ask him about this now that I think about it. Anyways, I opened his card and out popped a check for 2,500 smackaroos and written on the card was "take a trip". I had another out-of-body experience like that when I was told I would need chemo and also when Stanley proposed to me. I was overrun with emotions and almost couldn't receive that much emotion at once… because also we weren't really an overly showy family of emotion. I didn't know how to feel in front of them. I didn't know how to express emotion or even how to let that level of it in. I had to see the love in me to be able to feel worthy of receiving such love and kindness. It took work to get there.

We had love for one another but to say it out loud in front of everyone or to truly FEEL it – it just wasn't what we did naturally. One it was a shock that he would write a check to ME for that much and two, it was this feeling of pure love to know that he felt I was worth that even if I'd possibly be dead soon.... That even if I was going to die, he wanted me to have an amazing trip before I left this world. To this day, I think back about this other act of an angel in providing me love, hope, and healing through a gesture. It's not to say that money can save a soul. It's not that at all. But it is this sense I get that he knew exactly what he was doing and what I needed at a time that I didn't. Maybe he knew what setting sail and broadening my perspective and showing me a piece of the world would do for me. And at the same time, having someone believe I was worth it. Gifts can be given in different forms and gestures and this one really touched me. He saw me as a teen so he knew maybe I struggled with self-esteem. I think when one is so stuck inside of themselves – they can't even see a clear picture of life. But in look- ing back – I admired his humble way of living and his generous gift to me that Christmas.

I also remember taking a few phone calls and doing some research over this holiday season because Stan and I weren't sure about fertility or if I should try to freeze some eggs or what. I spoke to someone from the hospital about this and realized that if I decided to do this it would be an added expense to house the eggs, sort of like paying rent for an unidentified period of time plus delaying the start of my treatments and we determined that we had to let this go to God. I had always dreamed of being a mom to a girl, I had always dreamed of you Kirabelle. I never doubted how much I would love and adore you and that I was MEANT TO BE A MOM. But – my heart told me that you would come when the time was right and that right now, I had to first take care of me.

Something in me said to jump and take this leap of faith and let all the pieces fall where they may. I had to let go.

There is nothing like a disease to make one re-prioritize what is important and to put themselves and their healing first and this is how my "to-do" list went....

1) get better
2) see if baby is meant to be once #1 is completed.

I felt at peace with this decision. My mind could only focus on getting better – the rest I had to leave to someone else or it would be just too much for me to try to tackle and those feelings of overwhelm and weightedness would sink me not lift me towards the light.

My old to-do list looked a little more like this:

• lose ten pounds and then.....
• achieve my dreams and be happy

BIG DIFFERENCE. And cancer was my path to awakening to this. To awakening to the beautiful power of now, of self-acceptance and compassion and of building a life based on full embodiment and a bit more ease. It wasn't the easiest path but it was I think quite necessary in my growth and my transformation. You hear about the doom and gloom of the disease all the time and you feel the pain that can come from losing loved ones to it. And with each death, fear grows. On top of that with great attachment to the material world also becomes a greater fear of death. As a survivor and I am sure many survivors would agree, we feel those other stories – the ones of recovery – those spread hope and light and love. The ones where the body knows how to fight it and we need to let go. We need to trust. We need to connect to something that maybe we lost along the way....That stuff is needed and necessary during life. We can try to quantify it, come up with cures, but there is always a portion of it that will always leave us guessing because it is beyond human comprehension or control. To deny the spiritual or connection to spirit – I think can leave us a bit void and a bit at odds with one another. #LoveHeals

Chapter Three

Two Steps Forward...One Step Back

So Santa came and Santa left as he typically does each year and after a really great very present holiday where it was in my face how much family truly means to me, it was time to get my port put in so I could have treatments start. They recommended the port because, it was easier and my chemo was a slow infusion over forty-eight hours so I would go home with a bag (kind of like a fanny pack) as the drugs pumped into my body and killed any residual microscopic cancer cells (based on the three that they found). I remember texting my friend that had had leukemia when I was so upset to hear I would need further treatment. And he said it was great news. That they got the tumor and the chemo was just to wipe out any leftover intruders. To him, it was the last part of the war. To me, it was the scariest and I guess I was torn on the inside if necessary. Three teenie tiny cells and I was feeling so very healthy..... I was afraid. I didn't want that stuff in my system and I did trust that my body could fight three. I had been eating healthy and doing yoga and honestly felt it was gone. I had that moment of clarity after I woke up from surgery that I was indeed lighter and free of something. But, I also knew my family wanted me to follow the doctor's orders. I thought about not doing the chemo (I had started reading a blog How Chris beat Cancer and he opted for no treatment) and one of my coworkers at the time said that if he were me he would "double down". So I thought to myself – okay – valid point – good blackjack analogy. I mean this is serious. Life is serious. I wanted to fight and maybe I was scared of not knowing what it would be like and all of the depictions I saw on tv again involved puking and being horribly sick. Facing the unknown or fear often times builds one's perspective, confidence, and courage to later leap higher and dig deeper. You can look back and say "I did this" and maybe it wasn't as bad as I thought or had imagined. As long as I stayed in it and connected to faith and letting go – maybe this was another step to crossing over to the cancer-free side.

I remember one of the nurses who was there when I was getting the port put in. They didn't completely put me under so I could hear and feel some tugging but not pain. He told me how he was a pastry chef for twenty years and then decided to do something different and became a nurse and he jokingly said, "I wonder what I will do for the next twenty years," and I thought to myself this guy is interesting. He has a very unique way of looking at things. It is so not the typical you get a job and keep it until you retire.

Often times I love things but only for so long. I can tend to overdo somethings...except for my love of coffee. I haven't yet stepped into any boredom there. Every cup of joe topped with some fluffy cloudy froth always sets my heart on joy.

I remember after the procedure, if I would gaze down towards my right clavicle, there it was – my new roomie – Pam the port. It protruded from my skin and was almost like there was something foreign trying to pop out of my body. I was a little self-conscious about people seeing it but I tended to remember that voice in my head, the one that would remind me "it could be worse, I could have no hair". This is something a good shirt could hide. So I welcomed Pam as my tenant and after a year – I knew her lease would be up and she would move out and that part of my body would be all mine again. Pam helped me through each treatment and I was BEYOND thrilled the day I got to see her go. Til this day – she left a scar – a badge of honor that I sometimes touch …simply to feel. To feel the reality of life. It ain't always pain-free, Kira, it may not be free of scars, hey at times it may even be traumatic – but it is magically deeply profoundly beautiful.

It was about a week or so after that that my first treatment was scheduled. It was January of 2011. Stan and I lived about forty minutes from another branch of the NYC location and decided I would go there for treatments as it was closer than driving into the city each time and kind of near where I worked so I was familiar with the area. Often times on my lunch break when I wanted a treat – I would drive to this natural market and get myself something yummy and delicious now that I was on this path of healthy eating and yoga. I loved my trips there – so much fresh produce and an emphasis on nutrient-dense food.

Because of the impending snow, Stan actually booked a hotel room nearby so there was no way I could miss my first treatment. This again inserted some fun and adventure into something that wasn't so fun and pretty freakin' scary. The nurse was lovely and we entered our little cubicle where they would start the drip. My chemo protocol was a drug 5FU, a vitamin that helped it work and Oxaliplatin (another drug). It was a slow infusion so I would have a tube hooked to my port and then carry this little bag with the rest of it home with me as it dripped slowly into my body. Treatments were on Wednesdays and on Fridays, Doctor Stan – (also known as your daddy) would remove the port connection and I would be done. I would keep the stuff with me and return it at my next visit because it was too toxic to put in normal trash. It is quite ironic how you want to like the drugs because they are helping you stay alive, but you can't help but wonder how something so toxic helps?! But again, who was I to question this or so I thought at the time...yet I still did and do question?

The first treatment went fairly different than the puking and stuff I had read about and wondered if it would occur. They did a really good job of administering some other stuff to keep the nausea down and gave me lots of fluids to help flush it out. And I was a good patient. I listened to the "drink lots of water and rest". We went to lunch after and I ran into one of my bosses from my current job at a clinical laboratory. At first it was like I was so proud to be like "I'm done with my first treatment!" and I even pointed at the bag but then there was this awkwardness where it was like I wonder if he wonders when am I going to die? I wonder what he is really thinking? We went home and I had also gotten these amazing J.Crew pajamas. The kind where the shirt buttons up and matches the pants. I put those on and to the couch I went. Our dog, Higgens, was the best snuggler during the days of my treatments. I prayed and I knew lots of my family were sending prayers as well. This treatment didn't go too bad. I could do this. But what I didn't know was how the next one would go or the cumulative effects this chemo would have on my body.

Treatment #2 – Everything went fine at the infusion center and I remember going home. The worst part was the days it was attached to me. I couldn't do much, couldn't shower and felt pretty freakin tired. My taste buds were pretty jacked up too. Like a metallic taste at times. I did WANT to eat though – I guess this experience was different for each. It almost felt like eating real food, real yummy wholesome nutritious food alleviated some of the metallic taste bud taste that I would get in my mouth. One of the things I read also did suggest exercise which I normally really enjoyed but was pretty tired. I knew that I wouldn't always feel like going to the gym so we set up the treadmill upstairs in the office so I could walk. Stan unhooked me that Friday and he went off to work. I had developed a bit of a rash this time all over my belly and my arm. But I figured a rash wasn't anything to be TOO concerned about so I went upstairs to walk. Within a few minutes of walking, my tongue started to swell and I felt very very weird. I hit the stop button on the treadmill and quickly walked downstairs.

I was starting to have a hard time swallowing, it felt as if I could not get a clean breath of air. I dialed Stan's work number in a panic. I told him my tongue was swelling and he said to call 911. Later, when we could finally joke about it because laughter is well therapeutic and sometimes a good way to deal and heal…he did tell me that I sounded like I had a lisp or had been to the dentist. He immediately called a neighbor who was closer (he worked about forty minutes from home) to check on me. I tried to swallow Benadryl but at first I couldn't get it down. I called 911 and in the midst of talking to them I flung it back and continued trying to communicate as they asked me a few questions. I could not get a clean breath of air and I was really really scared. They said they were sending someone and asked that I put the dog away in a room upstairs. I tried to remain on the phone but my vision was kinda blurry and I remember putting one hand on the wine/liquor cabinet we had gotten for our wedding and thinking this may be it. I remember that moment as clear as if it was today. And I swear I can't write about that moment without 99 percent of the time crying. Crying at how close I got to staring my life in the face and realizing how ducking precious it was. That we aren't guaranteed forever and that people every day everywhere are fighting battles. In that moment I said to myself "let go let God" (something my coworker had written in a card to me). And in that moment, I completely let go to something bigger than myself. I surrendered. I faced death right in the face. And in doing so, I was flooded with something. Life. Peace. Breath. Something way bigger and way better than me. As I had let the fear of dying go – the rush of life flooded inside of me stronger than it ever had been before. And I felt it all.

The doorbell rang. I let the paramedics in and a man guided me to a step to sit down. He asked me a couple questions and I think the Benadryl, the surrendering, and the fact that help was here – I started to feel like I could breathe again. I asked if I could let the dog out before we went and I remember them joking that by his bark, they were expecting something much larger than my five-pound fluffy white Maltese and said he makes a really good protector. This made me smile. He helped me to the back of the ambulance where he started an IV drip of Benadryl that he said would work faster and quicker.

This man was another Godsend. He was an angel. He told me how long he had been an EMT. He was calm. He was at peace. He was caring. He told me his girlfriend had had cancer SEVEN times and was alive and well. He gave me another dose of HOPE, of humanness, of pure connection. He put a different spin on the deadly disease that takes the lives of so many. Seven times. Sheesh. I was impressed. Go human body Go! I arrived at the hospital and was put in a room. The nurse confirmed that I had definitely had an allergic reaction because she could tell my airways had been blocked and I could hear it in my voice as it was a bit scratchy. She also took some bloodwork and I remember her telling me I was really low in potassium. Okay – another thing I could do – go home and Google some foods to up my potassium.

Stan arrived and we went home. We called the doc to explain what had happened and then went in to meet with him. They arranged that I have my next treatment under surveillance in the hospital. Honestly, I wanted to quit. I was like I got two in, that shi* doesn't make me feel good. Often times, I felt like I could feel my heart trying to pump the stuff out and it was not happy. I would rather live five years than code blue. Was it worth it? But I had Stan and my parents who were proponents of continuing. Of listening to the doctors. And I get their side. I do. They wanted to do anything they could to solidify that I would live but the truth is – no one can do that. .....this is where the body is unique and an individual's decision sometimes has to be left to the individual to express how they feel. I think all routes have a place in this world. EVERYONE is unique. To say that you are protecting others by getting a vaccine but then overeating and overdrinking and being hateful to people or calling them stupid for not getting it – I don't know, dude? Unity and control over one's body are really important to me. Whether it be vaccine or abortion. You do you. Be your best self. Speak your truth. And I also believe in everything in moderation and you are your best moderator. Alcohol, prescription meds, green juice, online shopping – all of it. And I think medicine has gotten a bit out of hand in certain places – for ex. the U.S. Last time I looked at the CVS – every letter of the alphabet was full to the brim. The entire world of medicine is human. We need better balance. I am thankful the tumor was removed but I am not convinced I needed twelve treatments of chemo for three residual cancer cells. I have to do my own math. And I wish people would let each other without hate, control, judgement, ego and bottom lines.

Anyways back to the chemo – something didn't feel right to me. How could taxing my body more when it was trying to heal be good? Plus, I had been told that I was okay, that it was removed. I woke up from surgery feeling better. Was it the fear talking or my gut? Who knew better? Do I listen to the research and recommendations or was something inside me guiding me in a different direction. There are going to be times in life Ms. Kirabelle – where there is no right/wrong or good/bad – it is simply the right thing at the right moment for you and only YOU know. I wish I could know for you – but I won't always.

May you be brave enough to speak your truth and to follow your guides/angels/godsends. And may those working with you hear you fully and completely. May they not be closed off to listen, to hear you out, to see a different point of view..... We are here to teach one another. We are here to live in union because there are SO many people and places that desperately need help.

First, we met with the allergy doctor that was suggested (also the best of the best) who basically told us if it was anything in the chemo cocktail, it was probably the oxaliplatin and that there was this process called de-sensitation where they try to give you a teenie tiny amount over a slower period of time to see if your body does better with it. And the theory was the more you are exposed to it in a controlled setting – over time your body welcomes it. So we arranged a treatment under supervision with this protocol. They started it and then all of a sudden I remember them stopping it. I was breaking out in a rash again and she did not feel comfortable following through with this treatment. In the moment I was kind of annoyed with this, I was like just let me do it. I am here. It has been started. And I am drugged (they had given me Benadryl as well in the drip). What is the problem? But she didn't feel comfortable that my body could handle it and I am thankful for her discretion. Again, doctors are human. Medical research is full of the human factor. And well, things change, people change and while we are all alike, we are also different in ways. She said I was allergic. Period. End of story. And this to me was a lesson in patience. I wanted to get it over with because I was upset that I should be on treatment three and I am still on two. I am thankful for her. That drug was not for me.

So we left the hospital and awaited our follow up appointment with my normal oncologist. At this point he discussed my options. He explained that the main drug was the 5FU and that the vitamin they gave me with it helped it to stick. He said we could take out the oxaliplatin and in terms of survival we were talking +/-1% but he never really gave exact percentages unless I pushed him on it and even then he reminded me that those were stats and that each case is different. I really liked this doctor. He was easy to be around, he wasn't too stuffy of a doc, he had a sense of humor. I remember telling him that my taste buds were a little weird with treatment. I felt like I had cravings for Italian food and I remember him joking that his wife did as well when she was pregnant. It was nice to laugh. It was nice to not dread seeing him. It was nice to have a conversation with him as if we were two humans – here to learn from each other – not doctor/patient or sick/well or living/dying. It wasn't black/white – it was a beautiful shade of human grey.

My mom and dad arranged to come for this treatment and Stan and I were thankful for that. My dad didn't stay in the hospital at all but my mom was with me the entire time. She bought me food and made me eat it and she watched me while I slept. God knows what was going through her head again. From the outside she appeared no different than normal mom. But I wonder especially after having you Kirabelle, what would have been going on in my heart and my innards. She brought magazines and I remember her buying me this banana pudding. I ate it all and then took a really long nap. I remember that nap. I remember being so tired and I remember the way I felt having my mom around, in my corner, knowing she was praying for me and that I was not alone. I hope that I give you that feeling Ms. Kirabelle. It is a feeling that after becoming a mom, I want more and more to be around my mom for that same feeling. Mothers tend to nurture so many and sometimes the balance of filling up first is lost in the shuffle. Moms know this kind of selfless love. And I am sure some dads do too. But I feel moms in general know it more. You are a piece of me that I carried inside and you brought me so much joy before you even entered this world outside of me. Feeling your heartbeat so close to mine, wondering what you were going to be like, feeling the warmth as you grew and matured, knowing we were sharing our food and our breath. It was truly magical. It was divine. It was special.

Anyway, to get back on track....so we got through this treatment without the oxaliplatin and started to find some groove after hitting a large boulder. I remember being discharged from the hospital and my mom wanted to go by Panera for a cinnamon scone. Til this day, she is upset they don't carry those anymore. There is something about my mom and cinnamon flavored items that keep her going in this world. Bob Evans has these cinnamon chips she adores to put in her oatmeal and has now taken some home for her own at home inventory when she can't get out.

After having made it through this treatment and the after effects which again were made better by making sure to drink lots of water, rest, and walk LIGHTLY and do some things that made me happy like latch hooking or watching Ellen or snuggling with Higgy Boo. And I was very lucky to also have sweet and kind people sending me stuff and letting me know they cared. Knowing people are in your corner is amazing, I almost felt like not only did I want to live for myself, I wanted to live to thank each and every one of them for loving me exactly as I was – during the good times and the bad.

So the next baby step was going back into the infusion room for my treatments and being sent home with the bag for forty-eight hours. Treatment after treatment seemed to go by and I was gaining momentum. I remember in my head having the half way point where it would then be down the hill not up the hill and just like with riding a bike, downhill always seems faster and easier. Around the fourth treatment my friend Michelle offered to come from Virginia and she wanted to be there for a treatment. Her mom had had cancer so I felt like she knew what it was like and had experience so it wouldn't freak her out too badly. We went to lunch afterwards and I ate too much and man did it make this treatment worse. I am not sure if it was the extra stress I put on myself of feeling like I had to "be strong" or maybe feeling like I needed to entertain cause she had come all this way. It doesn't make any sense. She was there to support me. But knowing she came a long way and that her mom had died of cancer so this probably wasn't like going shopping with me, I wanted to be in good spirits and chat and stuff and when they suggested lunch I was like sure. But after lunch I went home and my temperature spiked, I couldn't stop vomiting and I wanted nothing more than to lay down. She drove home that day and I remember Stan and I on the floor of the "office" all night long. He just laid next to me. And I am forever grateful for his comfort that night….and well throughout the process but particularly that night. Do you ever look back and remember certain moments in your life so clearly…..those defining moments where someone else's love, concern, and care for you touched you so deeply? I hope you take time to reflect on those. Those are your peeps. Those moments are Godly. Those moments are spiritual. And when you can – to give it back – means the world.

Well this was one of those. The human power of love that Celine and all the greatest artists sing about and poets write about, it's true. It's divine and so damn beautiful that it's worth the pain that can come with it at times and it is worth the fight and the effort to sustain relationships built on it. I think at times we have all been touched by it but sometimes as we age we continuously think of the times that we were shunned rather than adored, the times we were ridiculed rather than complimented, the things we failed to achieve yet vs what we have, and turning back toward these memories always makes me feel good inside. Pondering them makes my heart full, full of JOY and gratitude. When

I stare at your daddy despite the fights that we have had – he is a good good man.

~~~

The next few treatments went without any complications. It got to be more routine and a part of my life or shall we use the term "new normal"? Change is hard, the transition period is sometimes the rockiest but once you get grooving, Kirabelle – humans are capable of change and adaptation.

Again, I was reading more about nutrition and getting deeper into my yoga learnings during this time. I bought a juicer, a Vitamix, a wheat grass maker and everything that I thought could help. It made complete sense to me that if I filled my body with the natural stuff – I was giving my body its best chance. I had a week off in between treatments and really enjoyed the OFF week. And I knew on treatment day not to do too much and drink lots and lots of fluids to flush it out. I also read this one book about visualization and did an exercise where you draw a picture of the treatment killing the bad guys or the cancer cells in your body. I have always been a visual person. Even now having had lived in Switzerland learning German, it boggles my mind the idea of Swiss German – an unwritten language. I need to see it. I need to touch it and feel it to really learn something, know something, and grasp something. I am sure it can be done though! Might be one of mommy's blocks.

Everyone at work was super nice and I had a work angel as well. She called me her work daughter and she was my work mom. She was the executive administrative assistant for the sales team. I knew who she was the entire time I worked there but we were never super close. The things I noticed about her were, her hair was amazing, I liked her clothes and she always had a smile on her face and appeared to be enjoying work. She helped me greatly through this experience and one day she shared with me her story on what made her so strong and such a person of faith. Before each treatment week, she would leave me a small gift with a card that said "Let go. Let God." The gifts ranged from like a notepad that said "live, laugh, love" or one time a candle or another time a bookmark with something uplifting and inspirational to keep me hanging on and fighting. To keep me hoping for a time better than the one right now and a light at the end of the tunnel. Her love touched me through these gifts and it was not really the gift itself, I was amazed that a somewhat stranger could be so kind to me. It got me realizing how much people cared about me and wanted me to be okay. When one struggles with self-esteem or their own self-worth, they don't realize the impact they may have on others – it is like I was too far down inside myself. And with these little meetings with angels, I kept feeling and seeing more love and light in this world. I kept being lifted. It was in a way, bringing me out of the dark innards or shackles that I had created and freeing me??!! The clouds were parting and I was able to let go of my want to be thinner, my thoughts about not being pretty or good enough, just to live each moment carefree because why not enjoy what all I had that had come to the forefront? It was all I was guaranteed and for some people I don't think they truly realize that until a near-death experience happens to them or a loved one. When the ground shakes, you take a deep hard look at the foundation of your home.

We all hear stories of how people had brushes with death and came out on the other side, often times better. More whole, more full of faith, more grateful, etc., I was no different and I was continuing through this journey of awakening. Things I used to loathe like my commute to work, I now found new simple joy in. I would be driving and listening to music and feel really alive and present, more alive than I had ever remembered feeling, or I would see a tree and the way the sun hit the tree and appreciate that moment of beauty with an appreciation I also wasn't accustomed to. The yoga classes I took were a practice in staying present in each and every moment to see the beauty and to take ownership of my thoughts, my feelings, my patterning, my reactive vs relaxed state, etc., etc. so that I could direct my thoughts and I felt brave enough to FEEL the tough stuff and remind myself of my strength, my courage, my grace, and my center.

Stan and I got to a point where we were able to make jokes about treatment. On Fridays, we had the option of going back to New Jersey to have my port disconnected or he could do it. So the nurse showed him how and I called him Dr. Clifford and he disconnected me at home, where I felt safe and sound and then we enjoyed a restful weekend. Not once did I ever see Stan express doubt during this entire ordeal. His positivity and strength are two of those qualities in him that I admire and aspire to be more of. Now through the years of marriage and becoming parents, he has also gone through some down times and to me, it made him more human to me to see that he could cry. To see that he could cry with me. Sometimes in society I think there is an emphasis on being Mr. or Mrs. Positivity and that once you find the light or the right exercise or the routine that works, then you have solved the equation to live a happy life forever. But I think life is more like a wave. It ebbs and flows and just like the ocean we don't have total control of the waves – only the paddle. I think it takes being vulnerable and allowing others to love you in times of need that bonds us, that grows community, that keeps us united. It is the human element of life and it is not realistic for any of us to think we can do it all by ourselves. We can aim to be stronger. We can learn coping mechanisms that don't require always turning to a friend. But, at the end of the day we are human and we need each other. We need community. We can't be siloed forever. And in my opinion, it is okay to cry. It is okay to fall on hard times. As long as you pick yourself back up, try again, and learn from whatever it is that gets put in your path. I also think it is up to each individual to figure out what works for them, what they believe in, and I firmly believe the best leaders lead by example not selling a formula to fix something and with an open mind that they themselves as a leader need to be prepared to shift and change as well. They lead with a deep spiritual connection, a good work ethic, and an openness that we learn from one another, and perspectives need to be relooked at from time to time. And while I can recount those moments where daddy helped me heal with love, some of the other moments where we cried together and embraced – those were uniquely beautiful and divine as well.

Chapter Four

FRIENDS... I'LL BE THERE FOR YOU....

NOW I KNOW YOU KNOW SOME OF THIS MS. KIRABELLE – BUT I MAY repeat myself here as parents do....

I grew up in Woodbridge, Virginia and never left until I finally travelled south to Virginia Tech for college. Go Hokies! It was still in state but for me, four hours was a LONG way and I remember my mom not being okay with this decision. She thought I would do better at a "smaller" school. The plus side to Tech having so many students was that it was easy to find a niche. To find your tribe as they say today. The campus was also very peaceful. The buildings were made out of Hokie stone (yes that's a thing) and they all had a certain similarity but yet different structure. The buildings encircled the drill field which I crossed every day to go to class. An open green area where in the summer, you could find people outside throwing a Frisbee or just hanging out.

So when Stan and I moved to New Jersey, I remember feeling like a fish out of water. I remember everything being new and scary and the Garden State Parkway was different in that miles went by and the exit number only went up one. I remember having trouble with directions because I didn't know what a jug handle was and it made no logical sense that I would veer to the right if I wanted to inevitably turn left. I also remember feeling awkward when someone else pumped my gas. For the longest time, Stan told me I had to tip the people so I always did. Now, anytime he ponders where all the money we made went, I jokingly tell him if I hadn't spent all those years tipping the gas people we would have more in the kitty. Ha! We lived in Jersey for about a year and then wanted to buy a place but buying a house in New Jersey was much more than buying a house in Pennsylvania, across the border and doing a commute. I was not a fan of the idea of a commute but we went looking for houses in Easton, Pennsylvania and found one, so we moved. Within a few years, we met three couples in the neighborhood that we became really close to. The reason I am giving a little background information is because these couples decided to surprise me with a "Halfway There" Party as I finished my sixth chemo treatment. And this, was another dose of love that I believe helped me along my journey. The men wore silly half t-shirts that they had made with writing on them. One said "Becky…1 Cancer …0!" These t-shirts made me feel like a fighter and they also looked ridiculously silly on our husbands with their hairy bellies hanging out that I laughed so hard that night my cheeks hurt. Everyone at the party drank and I remember being SO TIRED I laid on a chair at one point but I still enjoyed being in that ambiance and every now and again some intoxicated party mate would come over and spoon me or check on me or just ask how I was. The upside to alcohol sometimes (as it can go either way) is there are the sappy happy lovey dovey drunks who convey emotions and feelings they may have not been able to ever express sober. People connect. And this night, I was content in their love and their merriment. I knew they loved me. I knew they believed in me. I knew they cared about me. And I knew they weren't judging me. Or at least I didn't feel judged or felt sorry for. I felt human. Cancer to me has a lot of baggage associated with the name. A lot of history. A lot of deaths. And a lot of unknown as I mentioned before. But in reading more and more there are TONS of survival stories and tons of remedies and tons of coping mechanisms and tons of stuff not figured out yet. My attention was turned towards all of that – possibilities.

Anyways – these people – this tribe – were like family to me. They did not waver. I know they were uber helpful to Stan as well. They loved us both.

As the treatments moved along and I got closer to completion, we planned a trip away to the same place we had gotten engaged to celebrate. We had the Bora Bora big trip planned in September but this was a mini one since treatment ended in July. Friday the 13th to be exact. So my thirteenth treatment (we added one per the doctor's recommendation because of the complications with the oxaliplatin and choosing to take it out) was scheduled for Friday the 13th. The recurring thirteen did make me think is this good or bad and I kept telling myself – I made it! I am almost done. And if the 13th is the soonest I can do it…I am not going to put it off because of some rumor or character named Jason. That would be throwing away everything I had learned about letting go of labels, stats, outcomes in an effort to truly have faith, live in the moment, and do "me". Cancer had already taught me to let go and that is when the good stuff happens, that is when the well of life inside swells, that is when I feel a connection to the divine, to God, and to everything Holy Holy Holy – thanks Justin Bieber. Thirteen had just become MY lucky number…..

The last treatment came and went and Stan and I were off. There are only a couple of things about our weekend getaway that I remember as I do think the repetitive treatments had worn me down and it was now time to build up but I was pretty darn tired. I remember having a glass of red wine and it felt very acidic to me and not a good idea. It hit me quite hard. Maybe because I hadn't drank for a while or maybe because the chemo itself was tough on the body, that I didn't need to add another non-alkaline thing to my body right this hot sec. Maybe my liver needed a holiday.

I was sitting at the bar alone as Stan went to pee. And I randomly started talking to this guy. Come to find out he told me his story. He was a stage 4 cancer survivor with one lung left. He was having a glass of white wine and I think he was a little intoxicated. When you are sober – you have a sixth sense for those who aren't. Just like when you Kira would consume too much sugar and go into la la land and I'd be like dude, I'm down here. Anyways, we bonded on what having cancer was like and I listened to his journey. He races cars and because of his lungs, etc., he can't race like he used to but he has found ways to still enjoy what he loves and man you could tell when he talked about racing – that is his thang…it was a way he felt freedom and joy – being on that track in the driver's seat. The adrenaline or the blood flow or the chi or passion, whatever you want to call it – was there! He had not given up yet. He was living with one lung. And I was excited how the universe sometimes connects you with people at the right place at the right time and it was truly meant to happen, truly a working of God. I also remember him saying that he probably shouldn't be having another glass of white but he was going to. And in that moment I didn't think much of that statement but years later I understand the magnitude of the fear that comes and goes after a cancer diagnosis in terms of living your life. And from all the labels we put on things being good or bad. When something like sickness or death or trauma becomes real to you, when it hits you, there is an element of never wanting to go down that route again or to protect yourself just as there is in heartache. But the truth be that one glass of wine won't do it, staying alone won't protect you from heartache, and I will never be able to stop myself from suffering and neither will you, Kirabelle. And my motherly instinct will want to keep you from any harm but my deeper divine instinct knows that I have to let you experience your life. I have to like Glennon Doyle writes – lead you into the fire with a foundation of love, faith, and hope.

So in order to live a free life I have come to the fact that I have to be open, that I have to try, that I have to live as if I am living not as if I am dying or that I have to protect myself from anything "bad" or "toxic" ever being put into my body. Now with that said – it makes sense that I also have to commit to amazing self-care of what I do put in, when, and how I want to live going forward. I have to have faith and remain present and walk one foot at a time. I was touched by his bravery, his openness, and his courage despite whether it was wine induced or not that evening. He was raw and he was real, and in him letting his guard down, it made me more comfortable and had a domino effect on my being able to start to share my story – my truth – what I just lived which was really raw and really real and still often times can be associated with a lot of shame and blame. A lot of fight over what exactly cured me. What exactly brought me to be one of the cured stories and not the other? Or was it a combo? How did my healing take place? How did I get it so young? Etc., etc. I also remember after trying to drink one glass of red wine, feeling really tired and wanting nothing more than sleep and having a restful sleep that night, knowing chemo was over and this could be the end of my cancer chapter.

This could be the start of my next new normal. I had completed thirteen chemo treatments and only had a couple months until our celebration trip to Bora Bora!! Bora Bora had been on my list since Allie went on season 6 of *The Bachelorette*. Allelujah! *The Bachelor* and *Bachelorette* taught me so much about the world, travel, human nature, and societal constructs all in the comfort of my own home.

Despite the inner air of relief and light weightedness from treatment being over, it was apparent the treatments had taken a toll on my body. I got a bad sinus infection shortly after and I remember stopping on the way to work to pump gas and I somehow dropped my bank card and I bent down to pick it up and blood rushed out of my nose. The sight of blood and the sight of my body feeling weak and frail made me want to cry. The fight was long. The fight was hard. The fight was done. But healing….true healing…takes time. The memories of it all, the processing of it all, it all takes time. The treatments and the diagnosis had peeled a lot of layers off my onion and I had connected to my core but I still had a lot of rebuilding to do. From the ground up or from the yoga chakra perspective from my root chakra upward.

For the sinus infection – I remember going to the doctor and being put on antibiotics and I was sitting at a company dinner and I just felt horrifically weird. Luckily I was with two female coworkers….strong ladies who had made it up the corporate ranks of the company where I worked, where few ladies resided (at that time). And I didn't want to say anything but I felt like I was going to pass out. Being the recent "cancer" girl – I didn't want to scare anyone and I didn't want to admit to weakness in the moment but I did say something. They asked if I was going to be okay and I said, "I think so, maybe I need water." Once I got water and food in me I was better and I finished the dinner and went home. It has always been a fine line for me when to protect myself and when to not give too much without admitting that maybe I need to cancel a dinner or allow myself to say "no" and give myself rest and love from time to time. The truth is in most instances I find enjoyment and such appreciation for being alive and with others. But I also very much need and crave time to myself. Time in stillness and quietness and only me. Just me. But in that moment of admitting to vulnerability and weakness – it helped. And it passed. And I did enjoy the evening.

Around September of that year, Stan and I made it to Bora Bora. It was one of the most magical trips of my life and one of the most beautiful places I had ever visited. The water was SO TURQUOISE (your fave color, Ms. Kirabelle). We took a scuba diving excursion where the guide (who I swear was part fish himself) took my hand and guided me around to some of the most vivid, beautiful, colorful reefs I had ever seen. We got really close. And I wasn't afraid. I was at peace. Even the colorful "fire" coral. He made me feel safe and secure. He helped me to leave my fear of deep water for a moment – to feel alive and to see the beauty of a life fully lived "Under the Sea". And he intrigued me. He was a very small man who spent a majority of his time in the water. The water to me was kind of foreign. I didn't grow up swimming or around water. We never went to the beach. I did go to pools but in any large body of water part of me was scared, apprehensive and subconsciously I probably stopped breathing as well due to this fear. I don't even know if fear is the right word, unfamiliar? Unknown territory? Blocked? But he was able to help me experience something I probably couldn't have done or enjoyed as much alone and I had to trust him in order for this to occur. I had to trust a "stranger" but he didn't feel like a stranger. He felt like another angel put on my path to enrich my earthly experience. All I had to do was stay open. I think he was the closest I may ever come to meeting a human Mermaid... .or is it Merman?

We also did this photoshoot which was my idea and not something Stan would probably ever normally agree to do except on our wedding day. It was like for a couple hours I got to pretend I was a model or celebrity. Again, being a blonde female in love with pop culture this was my jam. The spotlight was on us and our love. I still have one of those pictures framed above our dresser in our bedroom and to this day, it still brings me joy.

The next few years went on with this being my new normal. I sort of lived in six-month cycles of some anxiety before scan time and then this amazing high when they were clear and I had another six months of not having to visit the cancer center. I could resume living and working towards my dreams. My then dreams being 1) achieving the cancer-free term and 2) having a family. Now let's go back to how during this cancer ordeal – my love of yoga came to life. I had done yoga before (at a gym) but I didn't love it and I didn't want to go back. I remember the teacher touching our feet at the end of class and my feet being very ticklish, I could not relax and thought it was odd she was touching my feet. After my diagnosis, I went with a friend to a yoga studio in downtown Easton where I lived and I absolutely loved it. I thought to myself after am I still feeling drugged from the chemo? Or did I just feel something? It calmed me. It relaxed me and I wanted more of it. I started going regularly and took a beginner's course to establish a good foundation. For eight weeks we worked through the basic poses and the idea was that after eight weeks, one would feel comfortable dropping in any yoga class and partially know what they were doing. The breath work amazed me. My 101 teacher, I will never forget him, his name is Danny and when he woke us up from shava-sana with his ocean breath, I felt like I had just laid on a sunny beach by the ocean. I felt inner peace and stillness that my anxiety-ridden self hadn't felt a lot prior. I also think in working my core, I estab-lished better posture and therefore held myself differently. I believe all of the poses help give the innards more space to breathe and move and maintain optimal health. This practice coupled with all of the books I read about nutrition and holistic approaches to cancer were helping me to feel better and better. Better than I had ever felt before cancer. People at work even started asking me what I was doing and telling me I looked "glowing".

At Easton Yoga, each class would start with a short dharma talk. Again at times this felt a little quirky and odd and different than any-

thing I was accustomed to and it def wasn't main stream to me at the
time, but I learned from these talks. During one, the teacher recommended a book by Max Strom, *A Life Worth Breathing*, and I quickly
purchased it and read. It was for me a quick read and an eye opening
one. Looking back, I think I lived the first thirty years of my life not
taking many deep breaths. I was def a shallow breather. In the book,
there are some breath practices and I would do those as well. Different
ways to count your breathing and different ways to control when things
around you felt unsteady – coming back to your breath. I didn't know
at that time that I was learning or adding tools to my tool belt to be in
better control of myself and my emotions and connected to my center.
To my peace. And what made this special is that I didn't have to turn to
anything or anyone. Because truthfully – this world can and will knock
you all around. I would use these techniques during treatments or during times when the diagnosis felt like too much. I mean don't get me
wrong other times I released through a lot of crying. A lot. And after
crying I always felt lighter, I felt like I had purged something that
needed to get out that might have been sitting there from all those years
of shallow breathing and holding stuff in. After I finished treatment –
yoga and healthy eating stayed with me. It felt good to be inside my
body and to appreciate it and take better care of it. As a youngster I had
dabbled with anorexia, bulimia, binge drinking, excessive running and
when I sat in stillness and moved my body in a very loving, accepting,
appreciative way – I got to know it on such a deeply profound level that
it aided and abetted me in my deeper healing.

Chapter Five

YOU WERE ALWAYS ON MY MIND

SO LIFE SEEMED TO HAVE HIT A STEADY ROAD. I, I MEAN WE, HAD MADE it through a huge hurdle and my body was gaining strength back and the scans were coming back clean so the next question was ....could I have a baby and if so, when? Being a mother was a DREAM of mine. Having a girl was something I pictured as young as the age of seven. You, Kira...You ...were always on my mind.

We had touched on this topic with the docs before and he told us that after two years that is when my chances of "it" coming back would go from like 25 percent down to less than 1 and then they would continue to follow me for five years in total before I was deemed "cured". So after my two-year scan, Stan and I decided that we would put having a child up to the heavens. Thus far, it had worked. And I was pretty darn positive it was still a possibility, more like a probability and I couldn't wait for what the future had to hold. I felt so incredibly healthy in body, mind, and spirit.

We planned another vacation, this time to Grand Cayman. Stan is part travel agent inside and he loves finding places to go and amazing restaurants to eat at. You have travelled more in your eight years on earth than mommy prob has in her entire life. Stan's aunt once joked with me that I was like Kimmy on that show where she is let out of a bunker and ends up in NYC bright-eyed and bushy-tailed and I can thank her for the reference I made earlier cause the idea often makes me chuckle when I find myself feeling somewhat small towny. Sometimes I fight him for control of this travel planning but it really is his jam and he is good at it. And Grand Cayman did not let me down. I remember arriving and I was tickled pink when our taxi cab driver's name was "Brown Suga'". And she did not say brown SUGAR. She left off the R and made it sound like it rolled off the tongue like butter – or wait butta? Not only did I love her name, I loved her vibe and everything about her. She was full and round and joyous and full of light with amazing skin. And she happened to recommend this place "Chicken Chicken" to Stan when he asked for restaurant recommendations and she did not disappoint his taste buds. Chicken Chicken was a local sit down but not at all fancy, more like a fast food restaurant with all these chickens they rotated on a stick and cooked with spices for many hours and served you with sides. Soul food. Warm. Comforting soul food. He loved it.

Another highlight was swimming with the dolphins. We did a dolphin tour where you could swim with a dolphin. She came behind you and nuzzled her snout into your feet to push you forward in the water. She was gentle. She was loving. She was amazing. And I think she was healing. The amazing thing about animals is you can take the animal out of nature (aka put one in the zoo) but you can never in my opinion take the nature out of the animal. Most of them even in the zoo live in the fresh air and they eat what they would eat (if taken good care of) on the farm or in the wild. I mean how many animals do you know who regularly color their hair or buy Burberry clothes or spray tan or drive around in Porsches or go to the gym? My time with animals and children have become much more precious to me. They are beings of light and they should be treasured for their ability to teach us how to love unconditionally and how to appreciate the simpler things in life and to not venture too too far from our innards. Something we as humans can get collectively away from.

And the last highlight I remember was a yoga class I took. I went on my own cause Stan was feeling like laying by the pool. I had made it a thing when I traveled to check out new yoga studios and I liked it. It was nice to see what the similarities and differences were and to experience different teachers. I felt amazing after this class and I did have an awkward moment after the class where this man said somewhat jokingly could have been partially pervy, "Now we all shower together" and I just sorta nodded and left thinking…yea, some of us do. Some of us do yoga and shower separately. To each their own, my friend. Stan and I went out that night and at this time in my life I wasn't drinking too much. This was a total change from college Becky. As I stated before briefly, growing up I was SUPER DUPER SHY. I didn't even want to crack a smile because I was nervous of the gap in between my front teeth. I know that one model made it popular but I didn't think I could pull it off. And I was pale with really fine hair and lots of freckles. I couldn't see the beauty in myself. I would just stay quiet smile and nod and every now and again I would find someone who made me comfy enough to open up a little and then I let out my funny. Oh, and I was always smart, or at least my grades reflected some intelligence. Then I went off to a college with 24,000 kids and no parents and beer, and beer became my world. I drank and partied as if it was 1999 every Thursday through Saturday and I was really good at it. Under the influence, I morphed into a social butterfly who didn't think I looked half bad standing in front of a mirror wasted. I flirted my tail off and even got the attention of some of the most talked-about bouncers at Virginia Tech. Oh Damian, how I still remember your smile and your biceps.

Now Kira – this is probably where your father and I will greatly differ in what we tell you about this period of your life when you explore your relationship to the opposite sex or the sex you are attracted to physically. And I find it interesting how women are more slut shamed than men. Let's all admit it. So this is another fire that I will gladly walk you into and let you go. I'll answer any questions you shall have and I will be there always. But I will not keep you from it – so please – be you.

Anyways, upon diagnosis I gave up drinking. I don't know if it was a conscious decision as I did all my reading on ways to fight cancer and alcohol being a "toxin" or if the treatments were so strong my taste buds and self couldn't handle it. It usually made me tired. Nor was I hanging out as much in places where people were getting wasted. Or maybe it was that there was this part of me that was holding on to every last second of life I had left and wanted to actually see and feel everything as clear as I could. The good, the bad, and the ugly. I wanted to truly feel it and all my healthy endeavors were leading me to this spot where I could safely feel all of it. Where I could fully be in my body riding this wave of life. All of it. This was life. And I was now quite confident in my ability to feel the feels and still feel okay. There was no longer a want to hide or shut down or tame any feelings. I wanted to soak in the moments of being fully present and alive. Years later – I think this was my time to truly look at my connection and relationship with alcohol by taking a break from it. My relationship with alcohol and my body is much healthier now having taken a step back to explore it.

Anyways so that night I had a drink – it was a mixed concoction with elderberry liquor and man it gave me the happiest buzz. We walked home a long way stopping and listening to some street music and just being young and carefree and in love. Stan and I's love for one another did not waver during this battle. In fact, it grew. It grew deep. It felt deep. Your daddy's love is one of my greatest life's blessings.

We came back from Grand Cayman and the good times rolled on. Stan was away for either a guys' trip or a work thing I can't recall and that weekend I went to the Easton Garlic Festival with our neighbor couple that I was friends with. The garlic festival is an annual thing in Easton and you can try garlic everything. Chocolate-covered garlic, garlic ice cream, soups, stews, etc. In the center, they had this garlic tasting contest where you could pay a certain amount of money to sample garlic from different nearby farmers. Raw Garlic. I mean in all of my reading I knew garlic was medicinal so why not have at it? And Stan was away so I mean who cared about my breath being stank? Garlic was one of the things I did cook with a lot of and Stan would come home from work sometimes and ask how many cloves I used today, and I would be like "it's medicinal" and tell him I was healing myself and he would laugh and then back away with slow caution. LOL!

Well this day I noticed something odd. I had way too much raw garlic and then a coffee and I came home and laid on the couch and I don't know if it was the coffee or the garlic or maybe someone liked to grow their garlic with a little something else or I was just sensitive shall we say, but I felt like I was tripping. I laid on the couch thinking I was like floating or high and I needed to come down from this. I didn't realize that is the day that maybe just maybe is when I started to feel the workings of you.

Anyways a week later I also felt a soreness in my boobs. It was a little more intense than period soreness so I decided I would take a pregnancy test. It couldn't have happened this quick? I remember trying before I was sick and I mean in five months of trying nothing had happened. How could getting preggo be this easy? I went to CVS after work to buy a test and of course I was standing in line and I ran into my neighbor friend who was a dude and not someone I wanted to share my current purchase with. I never bump into him at CVS. I quickly hid the pregnancy test behind my back. I still wonder if he thought I was acting unusually odd that day.

I went home and followed the instructions and the first test appeared positive so I took another to confirm. I was SO happy. I was so in awe. I was so alive. I was so lifted. I can't even describe the feelings that I had of nothing but pure abundance and appreciation for everything that had happened, for all of the love and care I received and for the chance to grow a human being inside my belly. This all felt like God's plan. This all felt like the EXACT WAY I WAS MEANT TO BECOME A MOTHER. I thought back to the person I was B.C. – before cancer – and I don't think I would have been the healthiest mentally or physically to rear a child but now I felt ready. Stan and I had recently watched a movie where at the end the woman told the man she was pregnant by giving him a little wrapped box of baby shoes and I thought to myself I will do this. I will make it super special. I will go out and buy a little cute pair of baby shoes and this weekend when it was his birthday I would give it to him and tell him. I think it was Wednesday and his birthday was Sunday or something like that. Well my impatient Virgo self – made it only ONE night. One long hard night of laying next to him breathing and feeling like I was in a straight jacket because I couldn't tell him. I couldn't wait to see his expression. I couldn't wait. So the next day at work I couldn't take it anymore and I emailed him. Which we laugh about. Because when we first started dating, most of our talking happened on AOL instant messenger because like I said I couldn't talk unless I was wasted or behind a computer. Behind a computer I also became a social butterfly who could hold fifteen amusing conversations all at once as I typed seventy-two words per minute and I was quite proud of these skills. The email that came back quickly from him made me feel emotion. Later he joked he almost fell out of his chair. Oh happy day. You were the light at the end of our first tunnel together. You Kirabelle – you.

Because of all that I had just gone through, I didn't want to share any of this until I was certain and until I made it to the three-month mark. I don't know exactly why but things were going so well I just wanted for us to be us. You, me and daddy. No outside world noise. I wanted to live each moment, each day and proceed one step at a time. Your daddy has always been more of a private person (on average). Stan didn't really like it even when I told people I had had cancer. He said the past was the past. Maybe he didn't want anyone to treat me or us differently? And I wanted to respect that. But to me hiding it felt like shaming it in a way? It was a piece of me. And why wouldn't I share? But this time we were in total agreement over this – that we wouldn't share until three months which would put us right around Christmas and we knew exactly how we would tell his mom. We used the shoe idea for my folks and for Stan's mom who would be elated to have a grandchild, we bought her a baby carriage charm for her Pandora bracelet and were going to wrap it and give it to her when we went to Colorado.

Telling my parents, my mom insisted she already knew. Plus, she had a grandbaby already so whilst they were for sure totally happy – it wasn't a first. Being the last of four, I often felt like this – as if the celebrations for getting my driver's license, or diploma had already been done. I often wished I was one of the elder children so I could somehow shine for my parents. The one thing I did that I think my dad loved that was different is that I played soccer on a travel team. It got him that sports thing that maybe some dads dream of. I had this friend in middle school, Ember, and her parents were very nurturing peeps. Her mom had this bright red hair and wore funky earrings I dug and her dad was like one of those gentle giants. He had a big belly like Santa, a dark mustache, and he was a soccer coach. They also owned pet birds which for me which was also a first. I remember my dad coming from work to pick me up after practice and if he arrived early he would stand behind the goal in his work clothes helping catch the balls of those shots on goal that didn't quite make it in. I felt like the experience of playing really did help build some self-esteem in me. I still never felt like that star of the team but I surprised myself in my strength despite my stature. At one point my coach was this strong German lady who was one of the sweetest ladies despite her somewhat masculine build. And she liked me. She nicknamed me Wheatie woman and she believed in me. And I now look back and truly appreciate the care she took to grow me, to help me realize my own potential and to remove blocks inside of me. Those people who are able to look outside of themselves, outside of cliques, and favorites and identify in each person what their innate strengths, weaknesses, and opportunities for growth are…. Those are the best teachers. Most of them probably have learned through tough times of their own and grew themselves into a stronger person and to me it shows the nurturing or female component of people – resides in us all.

So fast forward to telling Stan's parents – we were in their Colorado home with a nice fire going and the tree brightly lit. And inside, I was so happy. I had a really great pregnancy. I never felt so balanced and so full of light as when I carried you and about the first year after you came into my life. You were my sunshine. And I could tell as Stan's mom Marita opened that package, that you would be hers too. Now I am sure there was an element of worry throughout the pregnancy as I did just have cancer but the pregnancy itself and those nine months were pretty darn amazing. I read to you ALL the time and girlfriend – we didn't just read kids' books. We read it all. Every Oprah recommended book read, stories of hope and survival, fashion, friends, maybe some mystery.

I took a prenatal yoga class and did yoga up until about seven and a half months and was feeling great. I was working, taking care of myself, eating well, sleeping well and awaiting her/your arrival. I say her because whilst we chose not to find out, I always knew you were a girl. I felt it. There was a minor two-week period where I thought maybe just maybe Stan was right and you were a boy but that period came and went quickly and I turned back to all the cute pink baby girl clothes I had dreamt of buying when I became a mom. The fluffy, feminine, girly, gorgeous clothes.

I didn't want a shower which later I believe I realized may have upset some of the people within the family or had them question and the reason is I was content living each day and I didn't want to flash ahead. I wanted to stay present and sometimes looking too far ahead took me away from real moments. I had had the sheer reality strike close to home that life isn't guaranteed and whilst I wasn't at all worried about your health ever really, I just wanted to simply enjoy each day, each moment and spoil you with love not things upon your arrival. And I wanted to get to know you, to see what you needed, to learn together. Stan and I were very simple in terms of purchasing things for you. We knew you would tell us in some shape or form what ya needed. I think back to my wedding registry and I barely used half that stuff. I think I walked around Bed Bath and Beyond checking off the popular items like KitchenAid mixer when in reality I used the thing twice and it took up a great deal of real estate space on the counter.

It also seemed to bother some peeps at work that I wasn't finding out if you were a girl or boy. They were like "how can you not know?" and I just smiled, completely at peace with the not knowing although in my mind I knew. You had already spoken to me. This connection was deep. You were a piece of my love and I think the love of all of those that loved me through cancer. You were my miracle and I was enjoying every moment of this ride. Plus going to have ultrasounds with jelly goo rubbed on my belly surely beat having tubes shoved up my bum. I mean come on, perspective changes everything.

The months passed and your due date approached which by the way was filled with my new lucky "unlucky" number. So just like my having thirteen treatments that ended on Friday the 13th, you were due July 13, of 2013. I have contemplated this and to me I came to a conclusion that this was God's reminder that things can be bad and things can be good, it is all how you look at it. It is a training of the brain to look at things with less black and white, good and bad, right and wrong and to open yourself up to all possibilities of the now – because that is when you live fully and freely. It is also a part of life. There will be good times and there will be bad times. And no one is immune to falling on hard times. They test you, they test your faith, they test your relationships and with help, support, and faith – things can be overcome. I hate to say it doesn't always happen and I can't explain why. I wish I could tell you this. All I can say is that during those times, take even extra care of yourself and inventory of your life. Love yourself. Breathe. And put all that you can't control into the hands of a higher power. You choose that higher power. I chose God. I hope you do too but again, I won't force you. I do believe it is a truly personal decision. Life is full of variety. It is a true spice of life and it is not my duty to remove that variety or any color of the rainbow from your journey or exploration.

So let's get to my gyno. The man that delivered you. He is an amazing doctor that I found on the back of the church bulletin one day before you were in the belly. He had a very calm, confident, humble, caring demeanor. I started seeing him before my cancer diagnosis and he was happy to see me preggers. He never treated me differently, he never seemed to worry, he had the attitude that it was the past, and this baby was going to be alright. Now let me be real for a moment – it was a bit odd to see him in church sometimes. On one occasion he and his family were right in front of me and when we turned around to do the "peace be with you" I couldn't help but be a touch embarrassed. I mean this man has seen every part of me and now we are like staring at each other's eyes as if it's like "What's up. Peace". But again, perspective, in his eyes – he sees vaginas all day long and mine was simply one of them.

A couple weeks before you were due, you were still in the breech position which was a little concerning and I honestly remember the exact moment during my pregnancy you turned. It was in downward dog about four months in and I could feel something happening. It was crazy. And well, you never turned back. Now because I had done all this reading and basically completely overhauled my diet since cancer to eliminate processed foods, soda and all that.... I had dreamed of trying the most natural birth possible but again, God had a different plan. My mother-in-law was very concerned about this and I could start to feel her worry. She was emailing me all of these things I needed to go do like go see an acupuncturist who could turn the baby and I remember reading that email as I laid on the couch enjoying my big belly of love and I simply did not agree that this was a necessary course of action. I actually thought you were quite smart and I was okay with whatever you decided. I was like she (you) most likely checked out the exit and saw that there had been a previous detour and didn't want to put any more stress on that nether region and decided to come out a different way and I was cool with that. We were already communicating with one another. And to be honest, I was a little apprehensive as to how something so large would come out such a small hole. So we scheduled a C-section for July 9th in the morning and my doc reminded me calmly things could change but this was the plan.

He went away on vacation the week before and I was like "noooooooooooooo!" "Did you run this by me?" And then I calmed down and realized the man had a life and he does this all the time. That weekend though I did feel like I felt some of those fake contraction pains. What are they called? Braxton Hicks? What an odd name….But they passed.

Monday night I remember sitting on the couch with Stan and I was like "so, tomorrow we are having a baby" and while this wasn't the most natural of experiences we were able to snuggle and be okay with exactly where we were. We saw the positive in the being able to know exactly when we were going to have you in our arms and our lives would begin together outside of the belly. We had had a lot of training in letting go and in trusting.

Tuesday morning came and I turned into a scared little girl and called my mom from the waiting room asking her why she wasn't there and I remember her saying calmly, "You didn't ask me" and I was like "I haven't done this before!!! How would I know?" Anyways I cried and then I felt fine. She must have prayed.

They brought me to this table where I laid with my legs long and my arms out wide. I remember jokingly saying that this was like final resting pose in yoga and the one doc in the room from Philadelphia laughed while the rest of the room I am not sure got my joke as they remained silent. They may have not been familiar with shavasana. My doc was there and a girl who was training, a nurse, and the drug doc and Stan. I remember the entire thing. The girl had to leave because she got nauseous as my innards became seen by all and the doc was behind a sheet or some kind of barrier sort of like a mad scientist. I could see the top of his head and hair working diligently. He pulled out a staple that had gone from my colon surgery to my ovary and was amazed it didn't impact my getting preggers and then overjoyed he removed it for me as well and even showed it to me. I was also intrigued wanting to chuckle, anything else down there? Before he removed you, he asked me and Stan one more time to guess what we had and I said a girl and Stan said boy, and the doc said, "Momma is always right" and Stan's face went as pale as a ghost and I thought someone would have to catch your dad as he dropped to the ground but he held it together. I stared into his eyes with more love than I have probably ever felt between the two of us for having gone through some tough stuff and now to have this experience of birth and new life – man…it was like our love had moved a mountain. And it wasn't just us – it was strangers, it was neighbors, it was family, it was friends, it was not bound by religion, color, creed, or economic status. It was divine. And I am humbled and teary-eyed to think I was on the receiving end of that. Who would have thought cancer sometimes unites?

The other thing I really remember is that when my uterus was removed I had this extremely horrific pain despite the drugs in my upper right shoulder and I started to look at the guy to the right of me and told him and he said there is this thing, displaced pain where sometimes you feel things in other areas, he said it would probably go away when they put my uterus back and it did. This makes all that stuff about nadis, meridians, and channels within the body and what I have learned in my yoga studies something I have also felt. The body is incredible. And so is the ability to heal, how advanced modern, functional and holistic medicine has become and the beauty of when it comes together.

So that was it, now we had you! You were now someone I could hold and touch and kiss and see. Your face was so stinkin' precious and that pink cap they put on you like you were a mix of gnome and dwarf. And I ….I Kirabelle…was a mom.

It was like meeting someone for the first time but feeling like I already knew them. The breast feeding thing wasn't easy for us. My boobs were huge and dripping everywhere and at first you wouldn't really latch on. It was messy and it didn't feel so natural but after leaving the hospital a few weeks later you and I got better at it. We needed to be alone without interruption and we could figure it out. Your mom – she is a pretty sensitive soul and I needed space. I do remember Stan's mom continuously asking over the phone how it was going with feeding. And I remember her being a huge proponent of breast feeding and all I can say is, in my opinion it is like religion – it is a personal decision – and should be totally left up to the mother. There is no right and wrong in motherhood, Kira, should you decide to travel that route. The bonding period is precious and it is between mom, dad, and child. Mom can ask for advice if she wants it. It can be gently encouraged but it should never be forced on someone. I mean if we all went one route – where would all the breast pump and formula companies be? And while I just might have any attention of any employee of a breast pump company – can you please work on the noise level? Phones have different ring tones for a reason. That sound is enough to make one go bonkers who is dealing with minimal sleep, leaky boobs, and crying. Now there was a chance because you were breach that you would be born with hip problems and have to wear a brace the first year so it was refreshing to see you and your little legs not too stuck in that position. Another moment of gratitude and a lesson in we will let it go to God and tackle it if it comes…one moment at a time knowing the miraculous powers of something greater than us all.

The other thing we had not agreed upon before your arrival was your name. I mean a name is a big deal. People will call you that for the rest of your life (unless I guess you legally change it) and you will introduce yourself as such. What if you don't like it? What if it doesn't fit your face?

We had picked out some girl names – Kira, Zoey, Chloe, etc., and if you were a boy it was kind of a no-brainer. Your dad, Stanley Joseph Clifford IV was a tradition and how could I possibly break that many years of a name? It felt wrong. But it could be one of the reasons I subconsciously wanted a girl – the name Stanley to me always reminded me of an old man. No offense to your amazingly handsome papa. Now about a week before you were born I woke up at 3 A.M. unable to sleep and after watching an episode of the Kardashians I came up with your name. Kendall Hope Clifford. But, Stanley did not like Kendall. He says he could not grow to love it. He didn't know why. Later I learned there was a Clemson Tiger potential recruit named Kendall who ended up choosing another school and I believe subconsciously this led to his detest for the name but he will not admit to this being a factor. Because we could not decide, he eventually implemented this crazy point system probably based on some form of sports betting. We both had to list our top five and then we would add up the cumulative points based on rank and determine your name. Kira was my second and I can't remember if it was his second or first but it won. Later, the addition of Belle to Kira developed as I was singing "Silver Bells" to you your first Christmas and I absolutely adore this name☺☺ Kirabelle – I feel love and joy in my heart every time I say it and of course when I sing it too. And your papa and I are elated to be your parents. From the beginning until now (you were five when I first wrote this and now almost eight that I am editing it) you have brought true light and personality into our lives. You are a daily inspiration that reminds me to stay true to who I am, to dance in the rain, to hold my head high and let my belly stick out, and love with all of my heart this precious world and the people around. So – thank you, thank you for that!

I remember driving home with you when it was time to leave the hospital and Stan was driving and I have never seen your dad so nervous. We had this precious cargo in the back seat. I remember going over a bump and he yelled and then his first instinctual concern was to check on you. It was then I knew that I was not quite as important☺ I mean I was but I wasn't. So I joked with him never mind your wife that just had surgery and he laughed. We stopped at the grocery store because we were desperately in need of groceries and he accidentally started putting items in another lady's cart and she politely pointed out to him that that was her cart and he sheepishly laughed and removed his items. We were obviously still in shock that WE had a child. That WE were trusted to raise a human from birth to eighteen. That our lives had gone through cancer, he had a major job change, and now we were parents. Who woulda thunk?

I also remember your first pediatrician appointment and the doctor's advice was to first teach you day and night. So each morning I would take you out onto the back porch and say, "Kira, today is the day the Lord has made let us rejoice and be glad." And then I went on to explain that the sun rises and that is daytime and we are awake and at night is when we sleep. I may have been a little exact sometimes requesting and explaining the importance of all members of the family getting eight hours of uninterrupted sleep. While not all of this did sink in, I do know that you were pretty good. I would get about four to five hours and then feed and we would go back to bed.

Chapter Six

MOTHERHOOD UNEDITED

THE TRANSITION INTO PARENTHOOD WAS NOT WITHOUT BUMPS and bruises....and a LOT OF self-growth. Holy freakin' moly. I honestly think becoming a mom was tougher than beating cancer but Stan likes to remind me that when you are IN IT, it seems different than when you are past it (valid point). So, it could be because I am living it now but it is how I feel.

With cancer in ways, I received a lot of love, I got to rest, and I got gifts. And there was a clear divide where work ended and I could simply focus on ME. With being a mum, it is the most tired I have ever felt at times with a never ending list of things to do. Coming back to the yoga philosophy my root chakra (both Stan and I's) had been totally rocked and through you – it brought up stuff we needed to look at, heal, and work together on. I put a lot of self-induced pressure BECAUSE I loved you sooo much and wanted to give you everything. Like many parents do. I recently finished a book at the beach called *Real Moments* and it had some amazing pointers in there that true happiness comes from making sure you don't have a deficit of real moments. I wish I had stripped down some of my high expectations and aspirations to nap when you napped and to have even more real moments than we did although my practice in mindfulness did help tons. Plus, you Kira, had a way of always bringing me back. You had become the most spiritual ball of light within our ship and sometimes we simply needed to listen and to let you guide us.

Plus there are all of these situations that arise amongst you and your partner and your extended families when a child comes into the picture. A lot of healing can take place if we let it. Or conflict can arise. It is very much a realization to the parents (who then become grandparents) that the tide is changing and for some, that is hard to accept and I can't blame anyone for that. Who knows how I will be and I will be forever thankful to make it to that point. You are trying to establish yourself as a parent and listen to your gut but it seems parenting is a hot topic and there is a high percentage of people that in my opinion like to think they have done it the right way or figured it out and they want to "help" you by telling you how to do it. People would randomly share their opinions with me, even strangers and I wasn't sure if I had a sign on my head "no idea what I'm doing here" or "help" or I just looked nice and approachable. Regardless at times, it was overwhelming to me. I took parenting very very seriously and wanted badly to do a good job but being one that had struggled with self-esteem and security I didn't realize how all of these opinions at times would feel overwhelming or question what I was doing and if I was doing the right thing for you. ALL I NEEDED TO DO WAS LISTEN TO MYSELF AND NOT LET THE JUDGEMENT IN, BUT I DID AT TIMES AND IT WAS DUCKING HARD. Always trust your inner voice/guide Kira – she knows best. It is unique and special and it is the only voice that is right for you in a particular time and in a particular situation. And it changes. There is no right/wrong – there is moment to moment. I personally think we put SO much pressure on women to breastfeed, to work, to move feminism and equal rights forward – it is a LOT OF WORK TO RAISE A HUMAN AND TAKE CARE OF YOUR PHYSICAL, MENTAL, AND EMOTIONAL NEEDS. I wish sometimes we would all step down from the I got it right soapbox to the circle of holding hands and accepting our different paths.

~~~

I found the only way to tap into this voice is to carve out time to be still, quiet and ALONE and for any mother – this can be a challenge but doable. Through being sick I had cultivated this incredible self-love because my life had been in jeopardy and therefore I fell more in love with it exactly as it was instead of wishing for more and I realized that the more I filled up my cup, the more I could provide to those around me and the more it became refilled. It was like a beautiful divine cycle. It is what I think God wants us to do – to serve. To continually serve through our relationships, our work, and our community. And I can't do that without connecting to me and my higher power again and again and again.

I experienced this refilling with you one night. Stan and I were trying so hard to get some zzzz's. We had moved you from beside our bed to into your crib but you would not settle that night and anytime you cried – man – the noise I felt. I wasn't only hearing your cry but I was physically feeling it inside my body, we were so connected. One time at the airport – Stan had you in a bathroom across the entire hall and I could hear you. Anyways, it was a connection to someone so unique and so beautiful. This particular night, Stan tried a couple times to help you settle and then he would come back in and then five minutes later the crying would resume. We tried to let it go and see if you would cry yourself eventually to sleep but you wouldn't. My body lay there so very tired and so in need of some sleep but I rolled out of bed and took my tired weak body into your room and placed my hand on your back. I prayed. I told you how much I loved you and I just stood there. In silence, my hand radiating warmth and love and gentleness that was coming from some other place first. I walked away slowly and came back to bed and Stan rolled over, snuggled me and whispered, "What did you do?" and I said, "I filled up her cup." Inside, I felt my body overflow with love and energy. And snuggled together, he and I drifted off into a peaceful night's sleep.

Needless to say it wasn't always that easy or loving. I remember some tough fights and tough discussions. I remember wanting so badly to be able to express what I needed but it seemed like everyone around me had their own opinion and realistically with the addition of a baby – time and money are more limited than before. There is a new routine that needs to be established that very much emphasizes the simple things – sleep, water, and rest. I wanted to get some outside help and Stan didn't understand. He thought this is just what people do and that it is hard. I wanted to enjoy it. I did not want to lose myself. I wanted to admit that I needed help. That I could not do it all.

Our little five-pound Maltese pup also went through a tough transition. He had been my baby since we brought him home. I dressed him up, bought him Halloween costumes, held birthday parties, and pampered him with lots and lots of love and when you came into our lives, it was apparent to him he was unsure what this meant. We probably never meant to give him "less" love or less attention but inevitably it probably did happen. And less quiet time in the house. And he felt it and had his own way of getting back some attention, by running away. Now Stan still says he didn't run away, that he took a walk of solitude around the block to clear his head. But I remember it differently. My brother and his wife and their daughter came to visit us and Stan was entertaining whilst I went upstairs to breast feed you. I came back down and realized the door was opening and closing a lot with people going in and out and I said, "Where is Higgens?" and then fright came over me. I couldn't find him anywhere and I was panicked. Stan got on his bike and rode once around the block and all I could do was pray. The sun was going down and it was going to be dark soon and Higgens is so small – he could probably get eaten by a large rough bunny. I called my mom in a panic from upstairs and I was a mess. Stan came back and hadn't found him and then decided to make one more lap. This was the lap I always took Higgens on a walk usually. We had our routine. Apparently a house about half way around the lap had seen him walking on his own and brought him to their front porch for a little bit seeing if anyone would turn up. So they saw Stan looking for something and approached him and Stan brought Higgens back to me. I was happily relieved and reunited. Pets are so amazing in that they are so giving of unconditional love. This served as a reminder that he needs love too and sometimes it made the reality of the weight of motherhood seem heavier. How could I keep track of everyone, work, the house, and myself? I gave away two cats as a youngster because I wasn't fit to be a parent. Am I fit now? I had so many people to love and I was still working on keeping that love, strength, and confidence that I had found through being sick while also undergoing another major change in my life – motherhood.

At first I was doing well at home and at work. I felt like I was on fire, like I had this super power. This confidence that comes from giving birth – something women have that is so unique to the male force that controls so much else of society. My job was going well and people were noticing but in ways I wasn't accustomed to. At the time I worked as a financial analyst for a clinical laboratory. I started there as a pricing analyst even though I interviewed for pricing supervisor and then within a year I was promoted to supervisor. I took on a team of five people and

I had never managed anyone in my life and now as I look back at that time – I did the best I could but didn't know a lot about managing people. I was most definitely thorough, smart, and a hard worker. Most of my team had been there for twenty-five-plus years. To them, I was this young kid from Virginia who typed really fast and expected them to work hard and not complain. In hindsight I probably didn't understand the first thing about managing people or understanding where they were in life or in their own self-growth and then how to grow them and how to motivate them and how to choose my battles. How to connect them to that inner place of peace, confidence, strength and grace where things just flowed and oozed out of them – how to figure out the right times to pull vs push.

But in taking a step back from that career and then being a full-time mother/home keeper – I have thought back to a lot of what I could have done and to how much BETTER of a boss I would be now. Anyways in the thick of it, I started to completely feel overwhelmed and that is when I talked to Stan about getting help but he didn't really understand. His perspective was that it IS hard and this is just what people do. So I told my boss I no longer wanted to manage people. To be honest I am a very sensitive individual and at times I sensed their 'tudes. In some instances their 'tudes were warranted – one year the company decided not to give a cost of living increase whilst the upper management still got their bonuses. This made me mad but I didn't know how to say it. I was a feeler, not an experienced communicator. And my home life was already one rocky boat, did I want to work on one as well?

Instead of trying to approach this topic with my boss and express my worries/concerns, etc. – I just felt confused and overwhelmed. I got frustrated and didn't understand it – why things couldn't be easier? I remember being in a meeting with some higher-ups and this one guy on my team who would always give me the runaround and be protective of all financial information he had (even though we were on the same "team") – he said in front of my boss that he was going to send me some document I needed and had been asking for and I knew that he just wasn't because I had been asking for it for weeks. He was infamous at saying things in front of my boss and then playing some weird secret robocop control game. Anyways, in that moment I actually wanted to lose my shit, fly off the rails, yell, and fling myself over the railing. I literally was staring at the glass window wanting to do nothing but exit this room and be done with the bullshit. In my eyes, I could be hanging out with my baby – the most precious thing I have ever seen and I had to sit here and deal with complete immaturity. Sometimes I wish I had lost my shit. I think it might have been good for them all to see.

～～～

Can't we all just do our job and get along and have the best interest of the company and the people at play? I didn't like the "politics", I didn't like the game playing. And maybe partially I questioned whether I could have "it all" and what "it all" actually is? So my boss was fine with my going back to an analyst role in a new team that was working solely on big deals and joint acquisitions. He could use my knowledge and speed to analyze these deals and figure out why thus far most of them weren't working the way they were projected to. So I moved into this role gladly.

I didn't really miss you when I was at work because I knew you were taken care of and honestly my brain benefitted from thinking and being challenged. After the commute in, I looked forward to my quiet cup of coffee and checking emails the first half hour or so and if someone popped into my office to chit chat, I welcomed conversation with an adult. I think parenthood is such a major change that it helped to come back to the same gig, the same environment, and the same people. Speaking of the people at work even though sometimes I grew frustrated they were definitely like family especially through the cancer ordeal.

As you started to grow and going back to work was no longer new, there were times something in me was saying this was not right for me anymore. I needed to set sail. I needed to do something different. This role and this company didn't fit me anymore or I questioned my values and my compensation and my relationship with my boss. The more I studied yoga the more I fell in love with holistic healing and nontraditional modalities and the more I felt like they were needed in today's society with growing disease and economic and weather related issues. To me it was easy – the health breeds the sustainable wealth. The more you water your soil and tend to your tree – the better the fruit it bears. When emphasis is solely on money – some of that gets lost. It's like this collective imbalance.

The more I worked at this company it felt like emphasis was always on watching that bottom line. I could sense the frustration in the employees who had been there when it was small. They would tell stories about softball teams and work parties they had and how they worked HARD but they had FUN. And sometimes I sat back and noticed some of the similarities with upper management being that they used the word "busy" in excess. My dad used to tell me if he had a penny for every freckle I had, that he would be rich. Well, I felt the same way about if I had a penny for every time I heard the word busy – I would be a duckin millionaire but if you are so busy – how do you have such time to promote your busy-ness? And do I care that you were at work til eleven when I was home enjoying my din din? Do you want to hear about my fajitas I had? It was almost as if people wore a badge of honor for saying the amount of hours they put in at work. I had a HUMAN TO RAISE AT HOME. "I don't take vacation" was another comment that really triggered me. When a computer doesn't work what is the first thing the IT department asks you do to? SHUT IT OFF AND REBOOT. Like duh.

There was management pushing for savings and there were phlebotomists fighting for patient care and keeping the nicer needles for blood draws. There were times management would get together to find savings so that they could get bigger bonuses while the rest of us, our annual increases grew less and less. Would this not automatically widen a gap that already existed? My eyes were open to some difficult challenging parts of doing business and the current state of health care in the U.S.

This was so hard for me to find my voice and my place in this landscape. The fact that I healed and I knew what it felt like to be balanced or in the flow, the more I sensed when things were out of it. In fact, I was a completely different person after cancer and it affected all areas of my life. And if I did it, I knew anyone else could as well. But it does involve taking care of yourself (daily – putting in the "work" or "care" depends on how you look at it) and not everyone learns that at a young age. Not everyone has the same starting off point or the same opportunity or the same trauma. So I wanted to teach what I knew in a way that could feel more authentic. I thought if we could be proactive in taking care of ourselves, more energy could be poured into things like education and helping develop lower-income areas. I thought if we spent time grooming each employee and giving them the opportunity to excel and the environment to be motivated, have fun and work hard, the results or the fruit would then come. And there was some anger in me towards this dominant masculine energy. I wondered if the U.S. wouldn't have such a high incidence of heart disease and cancer if doctors were speaking about nutrition more and stress reduction and prescribing pills only when necessary...if it wasn't such a "do do" society and if the major large corporate companies didn't operate at a pace not sustainable and were giving back MORE. Large corporations used to donate so much more money. What on earth happened?

Prior to my diagnosis my boss and I had a great relationship. He was funny, smart, witty, and commanded a lot of respect from others. He was also one that didn't say too much and kept a lot close to his chest or is it a vest? Is that the saying? He asked me for something and I did it. I was a quick provider of information and boy was I fast and I did know my stuff. He trusted me and I would be quick to tell him who I believed and who I thought was iffy in their story telling when it came to sales. Basically I showed him the numbers and analyzed what he wanted so that he could make decisions and handle sales. And this worked. But the second I grew as a person and started to challenge things, we at times butted heads. And it wasn't so much with words, it was something I energetically felt. One time he even got so irate in his demeanor I actually put my hands up weirdly to block his nastiness. It was something I felt. Granted looking back the man was probably under a lot of pressure and had his own patterning to break. Who knows? I am not telling this story to say he was a bad boss or a bad man. I believe that he loved me like a daughter but that as I grew stronger and maybe my life circumstances grew me into someone he could learn from or that was quietly powerful, he didn't know how to be with me. He didn't know how to step outside the box with me. We didn't know how to communicate to each other. It is funny that sometimes we take safety in our roles and stepping outside of them to be human to human is necessary. It has been an interesting dynamic in my life with men and women in the corporate world. I think some say you can't generalize but at times I think you can. Men have innate strengths and so do women. I want to be respected for what I bring to the table even if it's different. I want to be heard for what I have to say even if it's outside the norm. With yoga, this made sense when I learned about the masculine and feminine energies within the body. It is not to say that we can't grow the other side or that we are all born the same way and nurtured the same but in a patriarchal society where masculine energy was dominant, it now made sense why I would feel slightly out of place and at times not safe or comfortable in a predominantly all white boys club at work and be frustrated by this as I wanted to be seen and heard. It appeared the more I healed and balanced myself, the more it threw some of my existing relationships really off kilter.

It makes more sense now after having had time to digest it all because as it happened – I just didn't know how to communicate how I felt, how to be vulnerable, and how to balance it all. With time, clarity came, resolution, forgiveness, and a lot of growth. Before cancer I was a complete Yes'er especially when it came to my job and tall white men that typically held leadership roles at the time. They were big and I always thought they knew better. Women were typically told to be quiet and nice. I abided by those rules for quite some freakin' time. Kira – know that it is OKAY to feel differently and to communicate how you feel. Always. Speak your truth directly from your heart and know that you do have power and you deserve to be seen and heard. Glennon Doyle writes in her book *Untamed* about being "caged". This poem speaks so true for both men and women at different times in their lives. She talks about resurrection and motherhood definitely leads to resurrection and so can fatherhood – if it is felt. If you take the time to feel it.

The small woman
Builds cages for everyone
She
Knows.
While the sage,
Who has to duck her head
When the moon is low,
Keeps dropping keys all night long
For the
Beautiful
Rowdy Prisoners.
——Hafiz

Thank you Glennon Doyle for solidifying and reassuring some of what I was feeling but never felt validated in feeling. You have rocked my world and tons and millions of others. And since the pandemic I no longer think this caged feeling is only applicable to one entity – it's applicable to the cages we put on identifying ourselves as female/male, black/white/Asian, adopted or not, breastfed or bottlefed, etc., etc., etc. My freedom and yours Kirabelle resides within. You will know when you are getting rigid as you will feel it in your bones and your innards. Don't abandon her voice. And make sure you are spending time outside of the cage.

Now part of this will be part of your journey or coming of age….as I didn't believe in myself and my voice enough at times to speak up and speak my truth and I had to learn to forgive myself for that… I would think of things I coulda shoulda said in meetings and get mad at myself afterwards for not expressing them but in the moment I was afraid of being different, of not fitting in, for being misunderstood…. I was afraid of saying the wrong thing, of being wrong or of appearing stupid. I also ran into my fair share of the pervy kind of men. The ones that would give me looks beyond a nice gentle smile. One time in particular I remember after being hired being introduced to some man from corporate and he joked to my boss that I was an upgrade to the last person who held my role and it was the way that he said upgrade that was kinda icky. Then there was another time where we were visiting a client in New York and had stayed at a hotel and this sleazy guy made a joke about what kind of noises were coming out of my room last night? Those instances I still smiled shyly rather than speak up. I didn't want to cause conflict. And Kira – I could hate myself for this – but I don't. I respect myself, I honor my journey, and I want you to do the same.

So as I grew as a person, as I healed, I wanted to be respected for how good I was at my work which led to some frustration with my current situation. I even came to my boss to ask for a raise and thought I had put together a really moving argument as to why. I had saved the company through my analysis and recommendations a boat load of money one year and to me this was a lot. Because I knew no one else could have picked out what I had. You had to understand the data like a wizard to help him see what we were doing in some of these agreements and it was all new stuff. But in his eyes, we didn't reach our target, it didn't matter how much I saved. He didn't think my work warranted it. And I just couldn't disagree more with this decision.

So I started contemplating about other things I would be good at. Because the other thing that really struck me after having cancer was the want to help people and to give back and in this environment, I felt STUCK. And I didn't like feeling stuck. It didn't feel like I was doing much at my current job to help the health of people. Also, my passion for taking care of myself through nutrition and yoga did not stop so I enrolled in the Institute for Integrative Nutrition and completed the course to become a certified health coach. Then I decided to also do a 200 hour yoga teacher training with the hopes of deepening my own practice but not sure if I would want to teach because that would involve public speaking which was like enemy number one on my list of things that brought up fear.

My fear of public speaking dated back to sixth grade Spanish class. I studied and studied and studied for this oral I had and when it came time to give it, I shimmied up to the front of class shy and probably staring at my feet and beet red and instead of saying "Hola" I said "Aloha" and the class including the teacher burst into laughter. Instead of taking that laughter as "I made a joke" even if I didn't intend to – I automatically felt shame. I felt like they thought I was stupid and I couldn't enjoy their laughter and share in it, inside I loathed with embarrassment and hate for myself. How could I study so hard and forget it? I went ahead with the yoga teacher training because it felt right. It felt like I was at a place to see that I was way too harsh on myself previously and that I could do this. I could face this fear. I wanted to grow this passion for something that helped me become a better person. I even joked during teacher training whenever we had to practice teach a class that I was going to move to Idaho that day. Another member of the training asked why Idaho? And I said I had absolutely no idea, it just came out of my mouth. Maybe from a recent trip to Five Guys where they list where the potatoes came from that day???!!

The 200 hour yoga teacher training was a huge weekend commitment and again I have to thank Stan for his support in my finishing. In looking back though it was a lot and maybe a little too much on my family at the time. It has been somewhat of a slow lesson for me to really see the importance of putting Kira, Stan, and Higgens first in every decision that I made and being realistic with myself as to how much they need me, how much I can give, and how much I need those outlets that still grow me and challenge me. Because mothering to me comes instinctually. It is within me. I started to lose a little of the energy that I had. I started to feel a little run down. I wasn't allowing myself the fuel that I needed to keep going. I was becoming a little lost as to what exactly was I to do with it all now? At this juncture?

Anyways even though I had these urges for a job change and was disappointed with my boss and I's current relationship I didn't know how to even attempt going about making a shift. I knew Stan was opposed to quitting a job without having something else. And the more I worked at my current gig, the amount of time I got to see you didn't sit well inside me. I had an hour commute so I saw you each day from like 6 to 8 P.M. and then on the weekends and I missed you. I didn't think we were getting enough time together. You were someone that I connected with and with whom I felt understood. You taught me things. You reminded me of the simpler things in life and I got to view the world through the eyes of an angel in your presence. I think at the time this was something I needed. I was starting to turn towards the bad in my life and not towards the blessings. There was a child rebirthed in me now as if I had been reborn that understood you more than I understood some of the adults around me at the time. I didn't fit in. But with you, I did. With my role as mother when it was just us – I was confident.

Now I know this chapter is called motherhood but I can't not talk a bit about fatherhood in this parenthood transition......

Over the next summer (you were turning one), we had a party in Colorado and invited two of our couple friends without children. This is when it became apparent to me that sometimes relationships can change and that motherhood is different. They were drinking, sleeping in, and during the day doing adventurous bike rides down sides of mountains while all Kira wanted to do was swing and play by a playground and be outside and all I wanted to do was catch up on sleep while Stan's mom was around and could give me a few hours of rest. It was also around your first birthday and I can't tell you how much as a mom I love your birthday parties. It's a celebration that I usually get to plan (with your help and ideas of course) and it is a time to sit back and watch the glee and joy of little kids and be proud of the work I am doing and whether this is selfish or not, I wanted the support of my friends and husband to take part in this. Stan's mom had gotten a cake to do a little celebration – and whilst I was thinking it was special…. Well, one of the couples had already left to go back to Pennsylvania and the other one decided whilst we were having cake to go outside and Stanley joined them. I felt awful. Alone. Really alone. Like watching me bask in mommy glee and celebrate one year was "uncool" for them. Like it wasn't a big deal. Like I couldn't expect them to at least fake it, just for me. Like someone ripped my heart out and like all things I have contemplated afterwards why it hurt me and whether I was warranted of these feelings and if this is a time, I wished I had found my voice in the moment and addressed it. I think not having a child is just as tough sometimes as having a child. It doesn't have to be a divide but sometimes it can cause cracks in relationships but probably the ones that already had them. Having kids is what some think society tells you to do, for some it's a box to check, but the reality is it isn't for everyone and it won't happen for everyone and if you don't walk that path, you won't understand what it's like completely but you can cultivate compassion for the other half and you can still take an active part in spending time with their children as an extension of them…..but only if you have the love and the time to give. My yoga practice helps me to find stillness and peace within that I want to share with fellow human beings – all human beings, regardless of their chosen path. In my eyes, it was a lesson to Stanley to choose me, to choose his family first, to know what was important to me and to do his best effort TO SHOW UP FOR THOSE THINGS. Was I overreacting? Was it fair for me to expect him to be there and not to leave the room whilst singing? Why did it hurt so bad? These are all things that go to show you that one human experience can be experienced differently by all of those involved. Brene Brown talks about it well in one fight she has with her husband where she is shaming herself on how she looks in her bikini whilst he is inside himself shaming himself for something he forgot to do for the kids or something completely different. They were so stuffed inside that they couldn't connect. I had envisioned this cake celebration to be one where we were all connected in how this blessing came to be and how connected we all were – but instead I felt a divide and I felt very lonely.

Fatherhood is also a major change just as motherhood. And Stan isn't one to always be open to talking or discussing feelings so this was new territory we were embarking on. But in telling the truth I believe only good can come. For dads, they don't have that connection of growing the child for nine months that puts them one step behind their beloved wives. They also have that societal pressure of being the rock, the strength and provider of the family but they have feelings too! Stan was used to only ever taking care of himself and as a child being the eldest male was taken care of a lot. He was the pride and joy of the family. Not to say their other children weren't. And there is still a piece of him that doesn't want to change his youngster carefree Kentucky boy drinking days. This is a plus in ways, he keeps me having fun but it also can get out of balance. One person cannot bear the full weight of adulting nor the full responsibility of parenting. It is my belief that each party helps the family when they can find that balance of selfish and selfless. Of nurture and of discipline. When they truly know their partner and what is important to them, what lights them up, what their core values are, and they get aligned on that. The most balanced children I think will be those that get to spend time with both their mom and their dad. Where both their mom and dad have present moments and rituals they do with the kids and they also have alone time. And I am not simply talking about duration but also quality of time. I read an article recently that the average dad spends about twenty minutes of true connected time with their child per week. Per week. Can you imagine the strength of a relationship based on that vs say two hours a week?

In a time where cell phones and computers and speed are so very ingrained in our society – children teach us to slow down, they demand it and if they don't get connectedness – how does one end up feeling seen, heard, or like they matter? They lose their connection to nature early on, to intuition, to simple fun, to spirit.

I told Stanley afterwards how hurt I was and how I felt. That when we were singing happy birthday to our most precious miracle and making a family memory, he was outside with friends because he probably found it "more fun" or "cool". I don't blame him for not knowing what I needed. I had to find a way to communicate and when I do in a calm manner, he does try to listen. We both acknowledge we have work to do and that we want to do the work.

Okay – sorry to sidetrack but you know how mommy does by now and I had to make sure I included that daddy had his own transition, our marriage had its own transition. It WAS NOT easy – but you, you made us want to both be better and do better.

~~~

So IF you ever DO become a mom, Kirabelle – know that it will TO-TALLY ROCK YOUR WORLD and your partner's world, but in the most magical crazy way possible. It will be another resurrection. And it might not be pretty. And it might take longer than you want to rebuild. But you do have what it takes. Give each other space and love. Don't be afraid to ask for help. Don't be afraid to cry and be angry and happy all in one day. Go with it. Let the tides take you. Don't get caged by anyone's expectations, opinions, or advice. And when you need help – bring that baby over!!

Love,
Mom

Chapter Seven
Bye Bye Cancer, Hello Switzerland

DURING TEACHER TRAINING, I MADE A COMMENT ONCE TO STAN that we should move to Switzerland. I had seen Switzerland on a list of the top ten healthiest and most beautiful places to live. Some days at my job, I would apply to jobs for a company my neighbor worked for that I knew had offices in Switzerland. I knew it was a shot in the dark like my dream of being an author but these ideas would pop into my head and I liked to dream. It brought me good vibes. It also was little lessons in letting go of yet another fear – failure. I can't tell you how many "crazy" ideas I have had on making money or how many resumes and applications I have sent in for jobs because I simply wanted to follow my heart in that moment and see. I wanted to get even better at hearing no and trying to figure out what my next step was....

Stan was intrigued when I mentioned this though because he had always wished he had studied abroad in Europe. His mom is German and he spent many summers and winters in Europe from a young age and holds many fond memories of those adventures. He took a German immersion program that he says was one of the toughest things he ever did but one of the most rewarding and bonding and memorable as well. Months passed and I never heard anything from the Switzerland jobs I applied for. Then one day, Stan came through the door after work and was like "Beckerson you won't believe who contacted me about a job and guess where the job is?" And I was like "hummmm…. Where?" And he told me Switzerland and we just kinda looked at each other. Like…woah…. Was this God's plan? Was this divine intervention? Had we been whacked over the head with our answer to what's next?

I shouted to the roof tops he should go for it. I was as I described having a hard time at my current gig and couldn't figure out my current situation and he had always wanted to go there – why the F not?!?!?! There was a piece of me that felt so thankful for him being there for me through cancer. I have heard of spouses that leave when shit gets tough. That is not the kind of man your father is. And I loved being free and taking these leaps of faith with him and now as a family.

Sometimes when the ship starts sinking, people in your life will jump. Mommy has experienced this as well. They don't look to grab someone else, they save themselves and get the f-out. But he selflessly stood by my side and took care of me and I didn't want him to have any regrets in life. We had both learned that life is short and we wanted to LIVE it. We also both believed that experience is more important and precious than belongings. And we both wanted to show you the world. All of it. To allow you an experience like no other. We also figured it was a good age. But first things first, I encouraged him to apply thinking in the back of my head, would this really happen?! Me…girl from Virginia who didn't leave Virginia until twenty-eight and whose idea of studying abroad was visiting the countries at Epcot Center… my family loved the Disney ride at Norway…living in Switz?! Cray cray.

The job was for a beer company which was another thing your dad adores…a nice cold beer. He was currently working for a candy company which happened to be one of my joys of life – chocolate. I joked that he could switch from my love chocolate to his love beer and knock that regret of his off his list of not having lived abroad. So Stan went through the interview process and I remember some of it was on Skype and we would joke that maybe he only needed to wear a suit from the waist up if that was all that was visible. (Little did we know later this discussion would be on a much broader scale with the pandemic ZOOM craze.) After a few weeks, he got a job offer and my mouth about dropped open. Holy shiz Stiz! We are moving ??!! Then I had to calm down and think this through because my five-year cancer scan was also coming up and this is the one where if all goes well, I am deemed "cured" and life continues without having to see a doc once a year or even step into that cancer center again. Now the percentages had drastically reduced, but like I said I had come to practice staying present and not jumping too far into the future, so we decided it was probably best not to tell his job and we wait for the last scan and then if it was clear, we take this as God's next step for us. We take yet another leap of faith.

I was a little stressed about this scan. It was big. I had already written a thank you letter to all those that had helped me through my illness and I had put it in my drawer at work about thirty days leading up until the scan. I had pictured myself hearing the words "you are cancer-free" and those words and dreaming of hearing those words made tears come to my eyes and this feeling inside that I had gotten over something really hard. That I was going to be okay. And that I was very loved and more loved by myself than maybe BC (before cancer). My good friend Joy (who is a godsend) and also came into my life at exactly the right time offered to watch Kira, and Stan and I would go into NYC for the weekend and then have my scan and celebrate. I wasn't sure this was what I wanted but I knew Stan wanted to go. Honestly it was hard for me to be away from you Kirabelle during this moment. It was really emotional. We walked around NYC and looked at the botanical gardens and I was trying to enjoy it but I just couldn't that weekend. And this is where I realize that in relationships, we get so connected which is great but it is that relationship with ourself that we also need to nourish and make sure is whole. So maybe in becoming a mom I had gotten a little disconnected from my center, my core, my independence. And whilst I think this happens a LOT, there is shame in admitting it sometimes. So I admit it to myself and to you now. I got a little lost because the me I knew was finding her new "normal". It was again part of my rebuilding or yet another resurrection. One that has probably taken seven years, a boat load of peeps and experiences, failed tries, and changes and I am darn proud of it all. Every drop of blood, sweat, and tears. Every moment of insecurity and judgement to come to this place of deeper acceptance and freedom and pride for who I am at my core, and for who I have always been.

The scan went well. Yoga had really helped me in the breathing aspect of being put in and out of that tube three times to do a CT scan. I had the same radiologist as I had had previously and I remembered him. I always wanted them to give a thumbs up or down as they were seeing the scan but of course procedure didn't allow for this and it had to be reviewed properly and in good detail before being given the results by my doc. I remember picking Kira up and that hug. OMG. That hug....that unconditional love of another human being so full of light and so precious. It is a gift that can be taken for granted by the parents in such a crazy busy world where we can't stop and see the light and just "be" for a few moments and bathe in it before we go back to responsibility.

We met with the doctor – I was given the ALL CLEAR and I was able to read her the letter. Now I wish it was my original doc I could have read it to, but he had moved to Florida with his family so I wasn't as close to this doc but I wanted her to know how I felt. I read it somewhat fast as I wasn't sure how it would be received and I cried. I cried tears that I felt in all areas of my heart and chills all through my body. Life could send you through a ringer but bring you right back out.

Cancer – you have taught me so much that I am grateful for, and I am joyous to say goodbye. To the doctors, many nurses, and social worker who treated me with care and compassion – Big Freaking Hug. To my family doctor that encouraged me to get a colonoscopy despite not fitting the mold of someone who needed one—Your listening, care, and attentiveness helped save my life. To the nurse who washed my hair after surgery when it was starting to dread – I felt comforted by it. To the nurse who told me a story about how she was left in her country to die from an illness, but she miraculously got….better… and sadly her brother who was healthy died tragically from a gunshot wound one day running through Central Park in NYC. At first I thought she was rambling and wished she would just take my blood, then weeks later – it sank in…and I want to hug her too. Life is fragile. Life is precious. Life isn't guaranteed.

After surgery, I was encouraged to begin walking and to the guy that raced me with his pole and the lady that did laps with me, I thank them. To the volunteers that brought this dog, Banjo to my room in the hospital, I loved him! To my pup Higgens for his amazing post-treatment snuggles and viewings of Ellen – I love you lil buddy. You may be one of the few I feel comfortable dancing on top of the coffee table with. To the stranger who saw me crying in the waiting room before my first chemo treatment and came up to me and said, "You can do this. I did." Her name was Gerri. And I thank her.

To my husband (also sometimes referred to as Doctor Clifford) – thank you for not leaving my side and for removing my port connection every other Friday through chemo, for helping me stay positive, for planning trips to make me smile, for believing in me, and for being a great father to our most precious blessing. To my family who taught me great values based on faith, hard work, and love, who visited, who prayed, who encouraged me that I could do this – thank you! To my in-law family who treated me like their own daughter – I thank you. To my wonderfully amazing friends who sent cards, wrote notes, sent soft puffy blankets, visited, threw a "Halfway There" party where the boys wore cut off shirts and their hairy bellies made me smile, thank you for being my friend – sung to the tune of the Golden Girls. To the people who reached out to tell me their story of survival and to become my friend, thank you. To both my husband's work people and to mine – the support was amazing. The food we thoroughly enjoyed and I still remember the squash casserole and these chicken enchiladas. My taste buds amazingly became alive during treatment. To my neighbors that reached out, I am thankful to live amongst a community of such great peeps. To my psychologist, your ability to help me understand myself and give me tools to deal with both my diagnosis and my life – I thank you.

To the acupuncturists, integrative medicine doctors, reiki practioners, expert massage therapists I visited, thank you for helping me remove blockages, move my chi, and teach me about healing….the deep deep kind. To the extensive community of yoga teachers and studios I have visited that fueled a new behavior and healthy passion in my life – I am blessed to have met you and humbled to be able to practice with you. Easton Yoga – you are near and dear to my heart. It is within these walls, that some of my moments of deepest healing and clarity occurred. To my fellow teacher trainees, I thank you for this experience and I am inspired by each and every one of you. Thank you for your support.

To the many authors of books on cancer, health, functional medicine, nutrition – I am in awe of you and hope to maybe write something...one day. To Kris Carr – did I ever tell you you're my hero? (enter Bette Middler here)....To my amazing gynecologist who treated me with such care, grace and compassion through my entire pregnancy and birth – I thank you. And it makes me chuckle to remember I found you on the back of the church bulletin one day. To my daughter Kira, for teaching and challenging me every day – you have a piece of my heart, and I want nothing more than to watch you shine bright baby girl and to comfort you when you do fall. Falling is a part of life. It is not how many times you fall, but the grace and tenacity you exhibit in picking yourself back up and trying again. To myself – I thank my body, my mind and my soul. I promise to take care of you and to continue to heal and check in with "me" from time to time and come back to my mat. I promise to embrace all of me, even the flaws. Diamonds with lots of cuts actually shine quite beautifully and need to be polished. I will continue to polish myself. Cancer – I am stronger because of you. To those currently undergoing treatment, I pray for you. On each and every morning going forward, I vow to carve out some time to reflect on all of those that touched me during this process. And to quote Ed Sheeran (whom I absolutely adore)...."don't you fade into the back love". Use_less._love_more

My doctor kept her doctor composure and reminded me to take care of myself as I finished my tears and the chills turned to warmth as I was done...She suggested that I make sure to get thirty to forty-five minutes of exercise three times a week and we parted ways. Then I went to the receptionist to give her some paper that the doc asked me to and when I walked up she asked, "So when is your next appointment?" and I smiled and looked her right in the eye and said, "I don't have a follow up" and she knew. She knew what that meant. I also for some reason though wanted to wait til I got off that floor to celebrate. I don't know why. It felt wrong to walk out screaming knowing what some people were there to face, to hear, and to endure. So then we got on the elevator going down and I looked up at my tall handsome husband and said …. "So…we are moving to Switzerland now?" And we smiled and embraced. A very loving present hug in which we felt every ounce of connectedness and love – love for the hard stuff, love for the good stuff, love for the unknown stuff. Love for it all. Love for this moment. Love for us. Both as individuals, as a couple, as a family, as humans. We were united in love and hope and a new beginning…in Switzerland!!!

So now that the decision was made, it was time to tell our work and friends. We thought the process of getting all the paperwork approved would take a while but it actually moved pretty fast. Stanley was to start his new job in October and I was going to stay and pack up the house, spend time with family before meeting him for Christmas in Colorado and then we would fly as a family to Zug, Switzerland – our new home on January 7th. What a wonderful adventure that was about to begin. So as cancer walked out the door – we opened our hearts to moving to Switzerland as our next obstacle course of life.

Chapter Eight

EXPAT LIFE

Now on to being an expat, oh boy, Kirabelle – where to begin.

I truly had no idea what to expect or imagine about moving countries. Telling our friends and family was a mix of emotions. We were met with some shock, some sadness, some "that is great." We made it clear we would be back in three years – it felt so weird to tell my family we are moving far far away and I know you don't fly and I am not sure when I am returning. Because the thought of leaving everyone we knew and the country we loved and were a part of was too much for me to process and commit to. I even wanted to keep our house and rent it out. Stan thought we should sell it. The market wasn't very good though and there were some items that we could not use in Switzerland – like my Breville juicer and my Vitamix that I couldn't part with yet. He had different attachments, one said bulky brown leather couch. He spent about 1,000 dollars on that couch about the first year we started dating and while it was comfortable – I'll give that to him, the thing was an eye sore. It looked like the two lazy boy recliners sandwiched together that Joey and Chandler sat in and wouldn't leave on *Friends*. To me, there was no way to be zen with that couch in the room unless you were in a log cabin in the middle of nowhere and there was a stuffed deer head hanging above it. It just wasn't aesthetically pleasing to my eye. He did not want to part with it so he convinced our friend that she needed that piece of furniture in her house and she kindly obliged but then later gave it to another friend because she herself couldn't get past its doo doo brown leather and bulkiness. Needless to say the adventure of growth in moving abroad already began with seeing what each other wanted to hang on to and how to make this more comfortable for the both of us and allow space for both of us to experience our process. I really do feel like moving Kira is like taking a plant and uprooting it and then putting it down in all new soil figuring out how to adjust to the new soil and how to nourish the soil. This was yet another resurrection or the next new normal. The process of taking leaps of faith, of standing on shaky unknown ground, of truly living. Of taking all you have ever known and leaving it only to arrive and put yourself somewhere else with not much that was really "known" or comfortable. To explore your individual patterning and cleansing that came up through setting sail and stay connected as a family.

Clearing out our house was a lot of work and also deeply cleansing. We had lived in that house for five years and managed to fill it with so much stuff and memories, it is interesting to let all of that go and feel the shift in you as well. When all of my possessions were on a boat and it was just me and a couple suitcases – it was like feeling super naked. It's like taking away a baby's security blanket or letting go of their hand as they take their first steps. In one instance – it can be BOTH terrifying and freeing. In ways as we age, I think it is also what keeps the chi flowing. I think Higgens even sensed that his world was about to turn upside down as he had another running away episode. It was short lived and I found him this time behind the neighbor's backyard. But it still was enough to send my heart up into my throat in panic. I just love that little guy. And I dropped and broke my phone screen three times before moving so I got to know the kiosk in the middle of the mall that fixes them pretty well.

Stan moved first in October. Ever since he took his job as a packaging scientist many moons ago – I realized when Stan starts a new gig – it is good for him to have space. He goes through a process and sometimes that process can be very unsettling to those around aka me and now Kirabelle. He cares about his work and at that time tied a lot of his self-worth to his job – so I thought it may be easier for him to do that without the responsibility and obligation of us. Plus, I wanted to spend my last holiday for a while in the U.S. experiencing the U.S. Christmas. Hobby Lobby decorating out the wazoo, Hallmark Christmas movies on repeat, ugly sweater Christmas parties, and just overall festive glee. Because as I stated in I think Chapter One – this is Santa's most glorious time of year and as a highly sensitive introvert – I am big on themes. They connect peeps.

January 7th, 2016 is the day we flew to Zug, Switzerland to make it our new home. The first thing I remember after an overnight flight is getting off the plane and getting on a tram at the airport and there was music on the tram that consisted of cows mooing and bells ringing and it sounded like a Ricola commercial. At first I thought to myself was I sleep deprived or delirious? Was this really happening? I felt alive and adventurous but also at times a little baffled that this was even happening or real. Somebody pinch me. And it was as if I was a kid in a candy store for the first time, a really big one. I also remember exiting the airport and taking that first sip of Swiss air – boy – did it feel different.

Everything was new so for the first year I really did feel like I was on an extended holiday in terms of there being a lot of new experiences and an appreciation for the cleanliness and health of the Swiss life. And hats off to them because I do feel like they have a strong close knit community with a lot of well-built individuals physically. The majority of the people that I would see around had a generally healthier look about them to me than I was accustomed to in America. Most of them still look like their light is on, like they are enjoying a good life, and they work hard and yet also stop to sniff the roses or take a glimpse of the mountains or the lake and they make enough to sustain a good life.

Another thing that really stuck out was the language barrier and its impact on my sometimes feeling like an outsider. I had never lived in a place where I could sit down at any random café and hear a different language often being spoken or where I would at times struggle to communicate with someone because of this barrier. Even in the states if I encountered a foreign speaker, it was more than likely Spanish and I had four years of that. Plus in my everyday world – it just didn't happen. Everyone spoke English and no one really balked at me for ONLY speaking English. After a while of living abroad, it was actually something I grew to be a little embarrassed by – that I ONLY KNEW ENGLISH and that I hadn't traveled more. Most people we came to know knew on average three languages. And some wore those languages as this badge of armor and judgement against those that didn't, aka most Americans. There goes that little voice that doesn't feel good enough. She's always in there – but the other one I was cultivating – she was getting louder day by day – the one that appreciated and loved me sooo very much and encouraged me to continue to be me and to show up in life as me.

I would have conversations and people would nonchalantly mention where they traveled last weekend and I would nod and smile and in my head, have no idea if what they just said was a country or a city or a store. And the accents did not help the situation. I remember one lady telling me she went to "Ikea" and she pronounced it "eye-kay-a" and again I nodded picturing this rolling green hills magical land not the furniture store that I grew up near and learned how to drive in the parking lot of. I say "I-key-a". Finally I realized she was talking about the store where you purchase build-at-home furniture and chuckled to myself. Now some days I could laugh at myself but other days I felt so insecure like I didn't belong here, like this wasn't the crowd I rolled in. I longed for sameness, security, and being accepted but instead I was sticking out like a sore thumb and sometimes taking it all way too personally. The days I stayed strong in knowing I was a good person and keeping my head held high were awesome, but it wasn't every day. It was like anything challenging – it was a process and I was getting really good at noticing my process and the room for self-compassion, self-care, and patience.

Even after two years of being there and a year of learning German I one day spent twenty francs at a photo machine instead of seven because I didn't completely read that the machine did not give change. Who knew that these little obstacles could either make or break me, make me miss home or feel challenged, make me wanna press on or take a nap, all dependent on the day and the amount of self-care and self-compassion I gave myself. Enter my yoga practice – as I stayed present I could observe these voices, these patternings, these samskaras coming back up again and again for a deeper letting go and healing to take place.

I also encountered my fair share of people that obviously did not love Americans with open arms and definitely had opinions about us expats. And when you are still settling in yourself, every discord I felt. Here my roots have been shaken and all I want to find is some comfort and stability and it isn't lurking at every corner. I gave every person I met and every stranger I saw a smile. But that wasn't always returned. My openness was more of a rarity. Flash forward though and I think it was the exact lesson I needed to be reminded of – how to be that comfort and support for myself, how to authentically communicate my needs, and how to continue to be ME even when it alarmed others. Stay soft even when the world tries to harden you, Kira, because it is that armor that can divide. You can be strong on the inside.

See – your mama is pretty energetically sensitive and at forty-one it now makes more sense than before. I grew up pretty retreated inside, introverted, being nice and quiet and observing life. I felt things. I felt when someone was actually happy or faking it. I felt when someone was looking me up and down in judgement. I felt when someone said the word American if there was some component behind it, some judgement, some discord. – I now realize this is one of my greatest strengths and at times a weakness when it inhibits me from being me and taking action forward. And, it can make some peeps uncomfy. Remember as I am writing there are some messages for you if along your path – you get lost or question who you are. Don't turn on your inner voice, don't be too critical of who you are and where you came from and what you bring to the table. Each person has unique beauty. Don't retreat for longer than a few days before you dust yourself off and put yourself back out into life. Being YOU is hard at times but don't compromise who you are to fit in. It is in those moments where I am me and you are you that we truly connect. Those are the real moments, the good ones, the ones that build an inner happiness and outer landscape not on the material plane.

I couldn't change the fact that I was American, I had to own it. And with each thing that occurred it could either knock me down, or I could laugh, chalk it up as a story, pick myself back up and try again. The more I stuffed though – the more tension arose in the body – exactly what I learned in yoga but was being stubborn to believe and often times wouldn't slow down enough to sit with it. Because when I sat with it – there was some discomfort and who has time for that? Well, my ego said I didn't. But my yoga teachings said I had to or it would build and I would go back to numbing in some shape or form.

I had some really amazing life growth from living as an expat in Europe. I had lessons all around me in dealing with others if I chose to listen to them and try rather than crawl in a hole and hide. This exact scenario – my finding my voice in dealing with people – was the same thing that I struggled with at my previous job that I talked about before. I struggled with speaking up for my beliefs and myself in times of conflict or with my boss when he wasn't energetically open to listen and this caused me to shut down. How could I live and progress if I shut down in the face of adversity?

Here I was stripped of everything familiar – all familiarities and I was left with me. Good ole me (and you, Stan and Higgens of course who also all went through your own transition). I have to say – you were the easiest. You took everything in stride. You were bounced around at first from a Swiss daycare once a week to then finally settling into an English speaking preschool. But you – Kirabelle – through this were that reminder that it could be done with ease. You didn't have any shame. That we as we age become stiffened and hardened and rigid. It is not our birthright. And through my studies of yoga – I knew that this could be accessed but it does require work and daily work.

Cancer was a great teacher and so were the Swiss Alps and as soon as I took some time to realize this and approach it differently and allow myself that self-love in the process, the easier it became but it wasn't without some stories to be had of course.

Take my neighbors for instance. The neighbors below us were Swiss…lovely couple with children and grandchildren. When you, Stan, and I moved in and they knew our furniture hadn't arrived, they invited me and you, Kira down for tea. We could barely speak to one another but energetically they were smiley, welcoming, and most loving. They were able to look outside of themselves to understand the magnitude of what a mother leaves behind – her village – to embark on this kind of adventure. They provided support. Now the neighbors upstairs – it was a bit of a less easy start to a neighborly relationship and it took us more time to understand one another.

Our pup Higgens had a tough transition. He was born and bred in Pennsylvania by a breeder who I think was also long time born and bred in Pennsylvania. He was used to a backyard and a house and he had this perch on top of our couch that allowed him to see outside at all times. With our flat, he didn't have this. The other traumatic thing that I think affected his transition was he arrived and within ten days had to get a health check where the vet told me he needed some teeth removed. She suggested we allow him a few days to settle in and then do it. And when she said a few days she meant a week so I followed her instruction and within a week of him being here – he was put to sleep and woke up with several teeth gone. Not a good first impression. I think back to what a silly move that was on my part. This transition took me much longer than a week! Anyways, he was barking anytime he was left alone and this did not make our upstairs neighbors happy. Now in my defense, he is about five pounds and I do not think his bark can be that bad because the insulation in this apartment building was pretty darn good. The woman of the couple came downstairs and basically told me this had to stop, that it "could not continue" and looked me straight in the eyes and energetically I felt threatened. I felt under attack. She did invite me upstairs and we chatted and she gave me a laser to try running up and down his back – light therapy. While this was a very nice gesture – her demeanor to me was still very much one of judgement and close observation of us rather than acceptance of our differences. We continued to have notes (in German) on our door every time he barked and whenever we would run into the husband and Stan would try to make conversation – he would utter a sentence back and it felt as if he had a serious problem with us. It got to the point where every time I saw them – I would tense up like oh boy what did I do wrong and it did not make me feel settled at all. It made me feel like I was supposed to walk around shackled and not free. Now I get it – you don't want a dog barking every day but I somedays didn't want the piano playing right at 5 P.M. – but I endured – wasn't this part of flat living?

Finally, one day I was coming home after taking Kira to a birthday party which attending three-year-old birthday parties was a lot of stimulation. The energy and excitement at the parties was off the charts... .something that after a bit of, I needed a break, aka to take refuge in my own home. So I pulled up because I also desperately needed groceries so I stopped at the store and I was carrying stuff inside with Kira and they stopped me again to register another complaint about my car door touching theirs and leaving a mark. Now from my point of view, I will never understand the parking situation in Switzerland or have an opinion that it works. Because as a mom with a small child – it doesn't work for me. The spots are made so that there is about a millimeter around each car and I have a child that needs to be put in and out of a car seat or requests to try to open the car door. Now maybe the spots are made to maximize green, reduce the size of cars and air pollution and encourage people to use public transportation or for moms to stay home with small children. Who knows. But I think a non-mom planned this and it is okay for me to find difficulty in it especially as a newcomer. But what bothered me more was the way in which I was being spoken to again. So I dug deep and tried to use my voice. The one that came from a place of wanting to get along, of wanting to enjoy living here and appreciating the beauty, the one that simply asked for a little time and space and acknowledgement that I was trying but that shit was different here.

That I was American but that I didn't vote for Trump and that I tried very hard to take care of our planet. So, I told her how I felt. I told her every time I saw her – it felt like she had a complaint to register and that I really was trying but that this was not easy. And I remember coming inside my apartment afterwards and feeling this sense of heat in my body....and energy....Like I had faced an enemy and come to a peaceful resolution. I had faced adversity and nothing exploded. That I had found my voice and spoke my truth without anger and in an attempt to move forward peacefully. That I hadn't allowed myself to be bullied or treated with disrespect and shove all that darkness deep down inside. Now I definitely think in ways, the way the community has high standards and holds one another accountable to high standards is great. And I honestly think this couple has positive attributes. And after all the yoga I have done I would say this approach of "walk this line this way" is more masculine than feminine. Just an observation from a chic from Virginia who happens to be super girly. I mean this approach has obviously worked (thus far) in terms of the stable economy and lack of poverty but I also think when you travel you see the conditions that other people have, the basis of life, the vastness and diversity of the lands they live in, and you cannot compare or ever hold the attitude that you have it all figured out or that we are all meant to fit in the same shape or sized hole. I mean who doesn't love the Skittles commercial about tasting the rainbow?

The second the ego takes over and I want to be right for the sake of being right and they feel the same – divide grows. In this case we were both able to put ego aside and melt the barrier in between us. To grow in compassion and love and as neighbors. And it felt right within. Both her and her husband engaged with us differently from that day forward.

Stan came home and I told him about it and he was proud of me. This situation had me reflect back on my career and my relationships.

I always wanted to please people and keep the peace and I backed away from situations in which I had an opposing view because I often saw a lot of different views, ways, sides to look at something. I am very analytical. It was the same with this journey into living here. On the tough days, I wanted to run back home to what was easier and on the other days I saw that I was becoming a stronger version of myself without the noise of anyone that knew me before. This felt like what God's plan was. For me to realize that I wasn't a broken person, that having had cancer wasn't shameful, that being "just" a mom was a darn good job, and that speaking one language was also okay. Being me was always okay. Being you Kirabelle will always be OKAY. Own your style, develop a strong sense of self and self-love and you will move mountains.

Now Higgens – this wasn't the end to his rough transition and a breaking point for mama – we had one more brush with death. I don't know about other peeps but when I moved to Switzerland (at first) everything became more of an energy exertion. Things like going to the grocery store were doubly tough with new long pin codes for ATM cards, new language, new aisles to become familiar with, etc., etc. I had to insert a franc to get a cart, etc., etc. So one day – you, me, and Higs had been out for a while and it was time to get home to recharge. You had fallen asleep in the car so I was carrying you, a bag of groceries, and Higgens was on his lead. We got in the elevator and I hit floor three assuming we were all ON the elevator. Well, the elevator started to move and I looked down to see the cord of the leash but it was going through the middle of the door and Higgens was on the other side. The elevator was moving.

My heart jumped into my throat, prayers started being said and you woke up and I promptly set you down on the floor and you didn't make a peep. We got off at floor three and I ran down those stairs to find Higgens sky diving from the ceiling of floor 1. He was hanging from his harness (luckily not a collar) with his little legs and arms a flailing. He seemed alright – thank God – so I took a quick peek around to see if anyone saw as I reached up and unhooked him from his sky diving harness. I felt like a total utter mess of a mom and a human. Who let me out of the U.S.? I almost killed our dog. I did get him down quickly and he actually seemed fine. Like maybe he enjoyed the short-lived ride of his life. I got up to our flat, closed the door and sunk into a heap of tears and horrid feelings towards myself as a failure. I called Stan crying. Crying hysterically. "I can't do this." "This is too hard." "I almost killed the dog." I have no idea what he thought. I know my self-talk wasn't kind or accepting. Who does this? Why do all of these other trailing housewives seem fine with these events as they unfold and I am a ducking mess? Again, how we perceive ourselves sometimes can be harsh. Compassion and acceptance – ongoing life lessons for me and require being mindful to catch myself attacking me and then turn towards a bit more love and ease for the journey, for the ride. Anyways, your dad calmed me down, made sure everyone was okay and I took a rest. Higgens seemed fine. You both looked me in the eyes and somehow communicated all was going to be okay. So after a rest, I then called my good friend Joy who was like me and I knew would understand. She and I chuckled about this because she later sent me a news clip of someone who had done the same thing and someone caught it on camera. Well, what a sense of relief – I wasn't the only one!

One of the other things I noticed right away about Switzerland – was the air felt so fresh and clean. I wanted to keep taking big gulps of it. And the views of the mountains, OMG. The scenery here called to me especially in my times of sadness or homesickness or stress or worry. There were many a day I would be walking Higgens quite possibly stuck in my own head as to how would I make this my life and if I made the right decision or about the bazillion things I had to do that day and all of a sudden I would stop. The mountains would call to me and I would stare. Stare at their beauty, their vastness, their perfect blend of strength and grace and I would be brought back into this moment, this moment of feeling really alive and really connected and really at "HOME". A home inside myself. A home that some live this life never experiencing because they are so connected to their physical home/ relationships/country. I wasn't a big traveler before I met your daddy but I grew to love traveling. I grew to love the change of scenery and experiencing new things from time to time. And by moving around, you tend to not grow stale of your surroundings but grow more in gratitude when reunited. These mountains were beautiful and new but to a Swiss person at times, it is all they have ever known and when you don't keep holding gratitude, then maybe it is not as magical as those first glances. For me, this was SUCH a gorgeous place to live simply based on its natural beauty and scenery. I saw their land through the lens of a child. This brought joy to both me and their country.

Now I enjoyed not working for about the first year. I enjoyed spending time with you Kirabelle even if it was hard because at times it was a lot of fun. You had this ability to help me see and enjoy the now and laugh and do silly things and tap into my own inner child. It truly did feel like an extended holiday. Stan and I travelled to Italy and Spain and we saw and took in so many beautiful, picturesque sites with different architecture and scenery. But it did start to feel like I was fighting with myself in my head too much about not having a paying job. Maybe it was my overanalytical Virgo brain, but I do think humans want to solve problems, and it felt like I needed problems to solve, something to do, a purpose beyond motherhood. I was feeling low again. Absolutely completely utterly lost. Who was I? How did I let myself become a stay-at-home mum when I so very much believed what was lacking at my last job was more of a female presence, more nurture, more care, more stillness. I put even more pressure on myself as to what kind of a role model I was setting for my daughter? And sometimes it did turn towards resentment towards Stan. Here he was growing himself and his career and he would be excited over how much he was making and I didn't feel like I had anything to bring to the table in that regard. I felt like I helped him make more while I was robbing myself of feeling whole. Yet there were parts of me that did feel staying home was utilizing my strengths – I was a good mom and a good homemaker. But I did question wanting more and that was OKAY! Plus, I felt like since we moved – the home responsibilities were no longer shared because I "wasn't working" and I hated that this was an issue. I feel like with all things if you do them every single day without help – sometimes you suffer burnout. Everyone needs a vacation. And I couldn't make Stan see that just because I "wasn't working" didn't mean he couldn't every now and again take the recycling to the okiehoff or make a bed for gosh sakes. But in his defense, he was going through his own transition. He was meeting new people, new procedures and the company did expect a lot, but his patterning was that he always had expected a LOT out of himself when it comes to his career.

It was as if we both were changing and figuring out who we were and wanted to be all at the same time, believing in ourselves and loving ourselves and being kinder to ourselves through the process and transforming into more whole healed individuals by looking at our own shi*. We had high hopes and expectations but at times not a lot of ease and stillness and fun.

Being an expat for sure rocked my world and I remember some words of wisdom from a yoga teacher at the Lehigh Valley Yoga Festival. He said especially during those times of big change, turmoil, loss – that is when it is even more important to keep up with your practice and a healthy routine. He was so right. Everything I turned to before during stress – alcohol, chocolate, shopping were abundant here but whenever I got out of balance, I knew. I was much better at moderating. I did feel a little guilt sometimes. It would hit at moments like when I went to the spa and lived in such a beautiful place and I knew there were peeps so less fortunate. I had a tough time of striking that balance of not beating myself up over not being perfect about it all. What did I expect from myself? What was there that I could do? Living a quality life and being grateful for what I had and at the same time using my gifts to help others.

I think being a "stay-at-home" mom (for lack of a better term) for me allowed the brain a lot of time for contemplation. After a lot of time on my hands and a lot of contemplation – I came to this conclusion. As we age and have much more responsibility – it can feel heavy and take us away from the light and from living. I can live each day being afraid of getting cancer again or wondering if I gave up on my career or if I am a good mom or the many missteps I made along the way or…… I can CHOOSE each day to do the best I can and focus on the things that make me feel good about myself and help me to put myself out there and feel confident and share my unique and special gifts with the world because that to me, is the truest most fulfilling way to live. I had to keep taking some sort of action forward. So rather than labeling myself as this or that or trying to find a way to fix something when I felt bad – realizing I am many things and they all ebb and flow. Some days I went to the spa and other days I learned German or explored a new mountain and they were all okay. I did start back up my daily yoga practice, I did increase my intake of vegetables and time outside, and I did develop a routine in which I was doing productive community building character building activities each day as well. I wanted to make sure I was somehow contributing to my new community and my core being and once the external noise diminished – my internal told me to stick by my child and my family first – the rest would fall into place in time job wise. They were the ones that stuck by me through thick and thin. And it was a tough lesson to learn that not everyone comes into your life forever. People wax and wane. Relationships. Habits. New shampoo. Etc., etc. But the root, the core that that yoga teacher talked about – healthy daily habits and relationship to self – so very crucial.

I read a quote about how sometimes you have to flip your existing world upside down to realize you were right side up. Sometimes you have to leave everything you know, to solidify inside yourself what is sticking and what doesn't. I did feel after being sick that my healing transformation touched those around me, I also had this·piece of me that felt like there was concern, worry, and a need to hold onto me and the way I was before cancer vs after in some of my relationships plus some questioning of my newfound beliefs in some alternative healing modalities and questioning of my judgement. And a lot of this I felt and then would turn inward and question myself and I would always come back to the fact that I was being me, authentic open curious loving me. I didn't think I had the answer for everyone but I was following my heart. I was doing yoga because it made me feel good not because I was getting brain washed by the Hindu religion. I was intrigued by how combining breath and movement was opening up my inner prana and cleansing my body and producing positive effects on my brain. And in my heart I believe that I could do yoga and still be Catholic and believe in God. Being Catholic was also a part of me. I was born and raised Catholic and at times I haven't agreed with things the Catholic church has done and at times I have questioned its humanness but it is also a part of my roots and my family and I wasn't turning my back on it. I was being my whole self. I was exploring all parts of me. I was learning. I was growing. And it felt right. However, the clearer I got – the more sensitive I was as well and I needed that alone time to make sure worry or fear or others judgement didn't creep in.

I now think moving was the only way for me to come back to my center. For me to stop trying to please everyone and figure some things out for myself. And for Stan and I to both figure things out as a couple and as a family unit. For me to spend time without work and with my daughter and with nature in this beautiful land connected to being and doing at a different pace than I would say most Americans. I had lost my way a bit and this was part of my beautiful, transformative journey. And again, not just for me, but for our little family. We became so very united in this process and much more whole.

One of the hardest parts in finding me or feeling worth as a stay-at-home mom or trailing spouse was reconciling loss of my paycheck, which was bigger than just a paycheck but at first.....it seemed like it must be the solution. I had to make money again to fill the void. But it wasn't the money – It was more of what I stated before – a purpose. However after you put out or exert energy – I was accustomed to every other Friday seeing a nice big ole credit in my bank account. It was a reward for job well done. And it did bring me validation to know that I was compensated. As a mom, I rarely got a thank you – although you do give the BEST hugs and you are a positive affirmation giver and mommy's biggest cheerleader now that you are older and I wholeheartedly appreciate it. I feel like we are in each other's corners celebrating our wins and hanging out to reflect on the lessons of loss or failure. As a mom, there was no annual review to discuss my accomplishments of birthing, growing, and laying down solid roots for a human being. In fact often times, moms are the worst judges of each other and I think it relates back to self-confidence and sleep deprivation and nutrition and some of those CORE items that fall by the wayside as the rock of motherhood is unturned. Instead of humanizing it with compassion – we try to separate stay-at-home moms vs working, breast fed vs bottle fed, the non-vacciners vs the vacciners, expats vs Swiss ....etc., etc., etc.

So to get out of my head and my contemplation of whether I was making anything of myself – I decided to use my teacher training and start teaching yoga. This would give me an outlet to share something that was really special to me, had helped me embody my body, learn about my core and stay with myself even through major transitions and I was meeting many moms in the midst of such. I had attended a couple of yoga classes at the gym here and it was really difficult to connect because of the language barrier. I would be cranking my head during down dog to see where the teacher was leading us next. It was not the same. I also found and maybe this was because at first I took gym yoga classes – that the vibe was more asana based – the poses. They didn't have the alternate nostril breathing or lion's breath or the dharma talk at the beginning where we all focused on gratitude. I liked that stuff!! Not everyone does but I really did. Exercise growing up had always been for me work and a way of pushing the body hard to achieve physical perfection. This was different. This was about accepting your body exactly where it was and then moving it lovingly as you shifted things around and learned where you were stiff and where you actually got in YOUR OWN WAY.

So I found a place to rent space and start teaching yoga. I made flyers with little paper slips with my phone number on them. At first, only about one or two people came and this was a blow and another point of growth. To teach from my heart and give my all to whoever showed up and the "success" was not in HOW many people showed up but if I could lead them to explore and enjoy their journey inside their bodies and to trust that the universe was giving me the exact number of people that was meant for me in that moment. Trying to keep all the self-doubt from not flooding in and proceeding forward anyways was tough. Was

I nuts? Was this too crazy? Was I good enough? Was I ready? Geez –
this voice was familiar – silence her! Does she ever take a vacation?

Then I found a way to advertise through an already established
forum for expats and seven people showed up and I got really nervous
– they were all from different countries and different levels. One man
was a complete beginner and one lady had just come from a retreat in
Bali and I felt completely out of my comfort zone. How do I as a beginner teacher cater this class to people more traveled who speak multiple languages and were at different levels? Why did I leave a studio I
loved and could transition to teaching at that already had students coming in?! This was too hard and at times, I felt so vulnerable. I wanted
to run. And so I taught a couple more classes after that and then I quit.
I ran. Because like I tended to do in the past – avoid adversity. I seek
comfort. I retract. But something inside kept talking to me as I worked
through settling in and a few months later, someone contacted me with
interest in taking a private lesson. She had seen my website that was
still up so I thought to myself this is perfect. One body. One peep.

I could teach at my flat where I definitely felt comfortable and I
could do this. It also helped that well, she was a really cool lady and
happened to have recently been diagnosed with cancer. She was part of
the secret club. I could help someone through their process of healing.
Part of the reason I was a little afraid to tell my story at times and to
give accolades to yoga for my healing was because of those that would
argue that. Those that would say well I had chemo too. And I did. Don't
get me wrong. And all I can say is I don't believe in one cure or one answer to a problem especially when it comes to millions of human
people. What I can say is that my practice provided me a more relaxed
state of mind, an opener heart, and a strong flexible body with a sense
of rootedness in this world that I didn't have before I started. I also am
a person of faith, I have great friends and family and I had the health

insurance to also go the mainstream med route and have some of the best doctors – so I was lucky. And I very much realize everyone is not as blessed in their fight. Socio-economic standings do affect health. This is a no-brainer. The world is imperfect and you may receive judgement in life no matter what you do Kirabelle because you simply can't please everyone. And when you stop trying to – and you own who you are and this journey takes time – it will be a milestone in your life. I knew in my heart what yoga did for me and I knew that I wanted to help people and this was following my path.

I also had dreams of writing a book with clear visions of what it would be called and that I was meant to be a writer. This seed was planted when you were inside my belly. It was another thing that was so very clear to me even though it was tough to say in the external world. Me as an author also made total sense to me because my verbal communication had always sucked. My thought process is way quicker than my ability to articulate in a way that is heard. But I am a darn good rambler and a darn good story teller and I have a very active imagination and also happen to be a really fast typist. So when those moments of clarity hit you as to your purpose Kira – listen – but also, don't try to rush or control the outcome. I am editing this seven years in. Editing this dream of writing this for you that has flowed in and out of me for seven years. Seven years of doubts, of distractions, of wondering if it would ever get written and if it would ever be read? If it could ever touch one peep?

Anyways, finding my first yoga client was the first nugget or crumb left on my path of creating my next new normal in Switzerland. The more Kira and Higs settled and Stanley settled into his job, the more I longed for something that made me feel like I could still do things to grow me and this was it.

Now in finding my "work" I will say I put a boat load of pressure on myself. Something inside me said if I stayed at home I was then contributing to the exact imbalance I felt existed in the world. An overly masculine driving force of the biggest corporations and largest money makers. In my eyes and in my opinion, Mother Nature is calling to us through this crazy weather, crazy pandemic, and it is saying slow down. One cannot physically work that many hours and produce that many results if not addicted to something – caffeine, alcohol, dessert, exercise – something man made. I think these things are great – if used in moderation but I often see a sea of addiction around me and less focus on child/home life. A sea of disconnectedness to what it's like to just be. A bunch of siloed people ordering Amazon and working from home never to connect in the way that they used to. And my yoga practice and my time with you Kira reconnected me to this thing. This thing that can only be felt when being completely present and still. For making time to get out of "do" and to "be". To spend time in nature. To get off the wheel.

Expat life also taught me some lessons on loving my partner through our individual journeys. We only had each other there. We met tons of acquaintances but when you are in the midst of moving and settling – I found it hard to truly get past the niceties to share deep stuff with others. I mean often when I was meeting people when you were super small – we were having conversations but also making sure Tommy didn't hit someone or you didn't bump your head or fall down, etc., as you were exploring life. It's just different in this stage of life and sometimes you don't stop to recognize it until the phase has passed. So to any mom trying to connect and share real moments while Sam is chewing on something he shouldn't or someone just soiled a diaper– that stuff is tough!

A few things I noticed and really LOVED about Switzerland as a country. First – it was super duper clean and kept that way. Even when they let loose for Fauschnaut – after the parade ended – two minutes later the street cleaners lined up to clean up most all of the confetti – I still found some in my hat later. It also seemed like everyone made a decent wage. Very few people actually went to college to get the kinds of jobs Americans have. A lot went to trade school or other professions that also keep a society running and they were paid a decent wage for it. The other thing I noticed was the drug store or apotheke – it was filled with herbs and teas and potions – not just meds. I dug that. Multiple languages were spoken at a young age with the children and while I don't think there is one recipe to raising a healthy child – I do believe this helps establish some extra brain patterning in the brain as well as guttural noises and sounds that create harmony and resilience in the body. I mean singing is great for this too and I am not a doctor but I believe learning and having a second language from the start – can be a good bridge builder later. Everyone's brain is getting a wee bit more exercise – shall we say? Lastly, recycling – at first the recycling center was a very scary place to me – I heard stories about peeps getting yelled at if you put the aluminum in the wrong bin but as I went every Monday (that became my routine) and separated EVERYTHING and learned when they made changes to what they were accepting and why – there was strategy to this that made me feel deeply connected to 1) how much I consumed 2) what kinds of materials and 3) their impact on the planet and countries at large. Totally dug it!

Anyways, as my teaching journey began and my quest to feel more fully whole – I also realized in this time that I needed to forgive myself for this wavering and to forgive Stan. He never means to become obsessed with work. He had never been a father before. I loved him and married him for who he was and I couldn't hate on myself for who I was nor expect us to be exactly like the other. I realized in marriage how important it was to truly acknowledge when you were in a bad spot and instead of turning towards blame and anger – turn towards feeling it and asking yourself what you need. Turn inward not outward. Connect back to the source where you will see things more clearly and be able to resolve things much quicker.

As I saw clearer – the light bulb popped on that opposites can really make a great balanced team. It's almost like when we first snuggled together as young lovers, I felt like when we cuddled our bodies fit together like a puzzle piece. I was fighting that fit as I tried to find my new me. I was fighting my own happiness because of my own internal struggles with how do I get to be both a mom and work towards my goals. How do I stay strong and true to myself? For him, it was how does he grow the part of him that nurtures and listens and doesn't want to fix, just is there for me. How do I get him to see that loving me isn't financially providing all the time but spending real moments connecting with your family, checking in, doing something for our house. How do I go about following my goals despite what people think and stay close to my truest self? First, I had to start by loving him exactly as he was and forgiving us both for any missteps we took along this transition. Now forgiving someone and truly being at a point to feel energetically open towards someone who has hurt you – those two things take time. But little by little as you got older and I turned my focus back to building me and honoring who he was– I started to feel more open. It was not easy. And this is another thing I think maybe more couples than not struggle with when kids are added to the mix. How do I find time to love myself, love my spouse, work and love my children? It's a lot to juggle so if the foundation is not sturdy – well, the boat can rock. And many often do.

I had one of my good friends Michelle from back "home" help me with my yoga website and then I happened to meet some amazing photographers whilst in Switzerland to take some really awesome photos for my site. And as I worked with my first private client – I grew the confidence to once again look for a space to rent. To stop looking at what I didn't have (five languages and wordly travel) and focus on what I did have. A story. My unique story. My relationship to yoga. My wisdom and knowledge of the body.

I found a space to rent and the day before I was going to sign the contract – I got contacted about a finance job with a large global company that I had done the first interview with a few weeks back and hadn't heard anything. Oh boy – what to do here? Kira – in life – there will be MANY forks in the road. Many times that no doors open and then multiple doors open at once. My best advice here is whatever decision or route you go – know that it is not the end all be all but it is a next step and as one of my current fave yoga teachers Allie Van Fossen says now – keep taking imperfect action. Keep allowing yourself more space than a tight rope walk. Keep living. Keep moving forward. The breath may get messy but you know how to breathe.

My gut said that being so far from home and not having a lot of help with you Kira – I wanted something more part time and I knew a corporate gig would not be that. So I started to teach regularly at this space. I wasn't great at it and I realized that with any other thing in life – the more you do it – the better you become at it. And with teaching – it has taught me sooooo darn much. Not only have I had to truly accept my body as it stands up there in front of others demo'ing stuff, some poses which I am not perfect at or some I can barely do and keeping the focus on guiding people on this open ended exploration of exploring yourself and loving yourself in the process. Of making people feel safe to go inside their bodies and move and explore. This is totally my jam. Have you ever heard the expression "if you don't use it, you lose it" this is my approach to yoga. Use it all. Love it all. Honor it all from your fingies down to your toes because as life happens, as you age, the shackles can tighten. Don't let them. Nourish every bit of you.

Move energy in all directions so you can keep coming back to you, your center, time and time again until you know that center like the back of your hand or a really cozy sweater or your hometown.

As I continued to teach – I also got to learn a lot about what parts of running my own thang I liked and which parts I kind of didn't. I loved the marketing on social media. Instagram was my thang and I was living in such a picturesque, beautiful place – I often times didn't have to step far to be hit by inspiration. I also loved planning the flows and coming up with quotes or themes to connect peeps in the room. I didn't love putting myself out there in new places in an effort to grow the business. It felt like what I "had" to do but I don't know if it was coming from an authentic place or maybe I was rushing it rather than stocking up on those real moments. I remember doing a fitness fair at the international school and I had my table for people to come and talk to me. I did not enjoy this. It just wasn't my strong suit. I wanted people to come to class and I wanted them to get inside their bodies and love yoga and experience yoga but I didn't want to find them, to convince them, or to deal with any stereotypes that it's a religious cult, that yoga people smoke a lot of dope or that I can't teach it because I am white. I didn't want to deal with any of that. Exit left please. But again adversity as you go after what you want, as you follow a path, it is impossible to avoid. So it became about acceptance and again a way to focus on what I did like. I also think Stan learned a lot about me and my processes as I embarked on this new adventure. I had something to talk about in our challenges to put ourselves out there and to be us despite it maybe being uncomfy at times. We could relate in our growth and our humanness.

Now I also decided to do other things to feel purposeful and grow myself whilst in die Schweiz. I became an English Mentor for the Swiss Schools. It was an hour and a half a week or so and fit in nicely with my current schedule. I got to work with kids and take them through a writing project. One year they did an exercise in picking a topic and researching it and then sharing what they learned. The next year they actually wrote their own short story. And I got to be the guide to guide them through it. I met children who were Swiss and those that were multi cultural. I met ones that spoke English at home and ones whose English was quite beginner level. And I got to be in the school environment. There is something about a place of learning that feels very spiritual to me – it's connected to a higher good. It's a place people come to work towards that higher good – that of education. Knowledge truly is power and it is limitless. No one knows EVERYTHING. Never stop learning. Never stop being a student.

I also volunteered with the church we decided to join in their clothing donations store. I loved seeing a place where the women could unite, the moms could pamper themselves with lightly used clothes and I could see the brands that came in from ALL OVER the world. How cool? Well, this particular church was having a ladies' bazaar where we could share things we made or offered so I decided to ask if I could hand out some flyers for yoga classes. Now I have felt the church/yoga divide before. I have internally gone and looked at my own thoughts and feelings towards it and I have always always followed my heart. She said sure and then another mom in the group suggested I do a fifteen-minute demo or mini class to give peeps a taste of it. Well, this was met with some resistance. The lady who was organizing the bazaar had me in to chat and sat me down in front of the bible and showed me a passage that read where God is basically a jealous god not jealous in a bad way but in a good way she told me – in which he only wanted you to love and adore him. So she asked if I used words like Namaste, etc. This entire discussion didn't feel good to me. Who was she to question my faith or my relationship with my God? And at the root of God – didn't he love and accept everyone? Wasn't the basis of all religions human love and acceptance and about being a good person? And couldn't any passage in the bible be twisted as part of a larger story just like horoscopes? I mean I deeply believe in having faith and that my faith aided in my healing but through yoga is where I could actually connect to my God or my higher power. I couldn't even feel him before. I was pretty blocked. I was trapped inside my head and my body with not a lot of voices saying Becky – you can or Becky you are good enough. But when I moved and connected to my breath and spent time in stillness loving every inch of me and truly thinking about my programming – I healed on a deeply profound level and found some liberation.

It was in stillness of which I could not sit in before because I was at war with myself. And when people ask if I say another word or listen to music from another culture – I do. I say German words in Switzerland, I have deep relationships with people of other religions and my God thinks it's okay. And when I think about you Kirabelle – I know that you are here because of SO many people's love and those people are of all different makes, models, types, sizes, religions, colors, social classes, economic classes, and relationships. You are my miracle that rose up out of all those divides we try to create in an effort to control or hold power over the masses. But my God, Kira, my God, he teaches me to serve and to do things for a higher good and to not create divide but unity as we raise the bar higher so that we can soar higher and repair some of the discrepancies that have been created before us. In that moment, I did speak my truth. I don't remember if I said everything I wanted or as eloquently as I wanted but I did say that for me, I could still teach yoga and also be Catholic and pray to God. I also believe people can get a divorce and still love God, they can be gay and still love God, they can get an abortion and still love God. And God can love them. So once I had dodged another bullet in being caged and a life lesson in believing in me – I decided to stop volunteering there and it was done with an open heart. I didn't hate her for having her opinion but I also didn't buy into it. I was not going to drink this Kool-Aid.

My private client business in Switzerland especially started to pick up right as I was leaving. When we originally came to Switzerland we said we would stay three years and then return "home". While our definition of home was now different – I still couldn't picture you growing up without a solid relationship to your grandparents for as long as they were here on this earth to influence your life and be your mentors. My grandmother was such a solid influence in my life. I remember so many things about her and often times reflect on what an amazing lady she was. I remember playing Scrabble with her and how some games got quite intense. She was quite the competitor. I remember her love of Judge Wapner and the *People's Court*, Girls Gymnastics and *Jeopardy*. I remember she put her teeth in on Tuesday nights to go to Bingo and she looked so pretty to me when she put her red lipstick on. Oh, and I can't even tell you about her peanut butter fudge. Every time I want to connect to her – I find a candy store that makes homemade fudge – get a piece of peanut butter and sit outside and have a moment. I feel like she comes and sits with me every time. It's her and I's thang.

And I know my mom wasn't ever going to travel to Switzerland. She doesn't fly. And whilst this book is all about hope – I am unsure what it would take to get her on a plane – probably blindfolded and drugged but I don't want to get arrested. This plane may have already left the airport in her lifetime and I accept that. No judgement there. People are people as Nightbirde sings today and that is okay. People are people.

So now our lives have set sail and we have been opened to new opportunities and the beauty of Europe – but our hearts – called us home. Stan felt it too. He had started applying to see if he could get a job that would bring us back at his previous company as new company was going through another round of layoffs so the ground was unsturdy again. I was pretty secure that they were happy with him and he would be fine – but he wasn't. I even thought he could ask to move to NYC as they have offices there but he said those were for other type job roles. Anyways, he got offered a job that appealed to him back at the candy company he was at before so he was set to start in March and I wanted to finish out the school year for you and teaching for me. I wasn't ready to leave yet. Plus, if you remember when daddy starts a new job – it's good for him to have space to focus and transition and then we could join him after some of the dust had settled. So he left. I think a strong relationship can withstand some time apart. And you and I – we work well together.

We had a lot of fun. We spent a lot of time at the Badi getting our daily dose of beautiful gorgeous lake Zug and at the Baar Mcdonalds getting our dose of our home away from home and really amazing cappuccino froth and play area. Way to think of the moms. I was a bit sad to think that my business was getting a bit busier – and that piece of my pie was getting filled and it was time to go. But I had spoken to a studio back in Easton and thought I could continue my teaching journey and life journey back in Easton. We had gained a lot of confidence and self-growth from embarking on this journey and you Kirabelle had developed some really strong roots, a love of travel and new experiences and it had bonded the four of us. Plus, Higgy was elated to return back home. He had the toughest transition there but the easiest transition back....but let me get to that in this next chapter....as we returned "home".

Switzerland will always have a special place in my heart and I cannot wait to go back to visit.

Chapter Nine

RETURNING "HOME"

SO MY YOGA PRACTICE AND CONSISTENT TIME WORKING ON "ME" have brought me "home" time and time again to this place that lives and resides inside of me where all is good and all is aligned with truth even during tough stuff. The innards as I sometimes call it, they are in balance and dancing with the winds of life. Then other days or moments I feel a shift away from home, more into this automatic proceed forward "do" kinda mentality. So the U.S. was definitely my first home country and I couldn't wait to return to it. I couldn't wait to see the aisle upon aisle of nut butters and familiar faces and not have to speak German anymore as I never fell in love with the language. I could beat myself up by telling myself maybe I didn't give it enough time or I could just take it for what it was – I was following my joy, my purpose, my path. Who's to say I wouldn't feel joy to speak German one day? There isn't much I leave off the table totally because I thrive in freedom of all possibility. I feel more free when I don't create cages or end all be alls.

So being back was totally exciting because again, it was all "new" again and I got to be reunited with your daddy and our little family got to live in our blue house again. You again seemed to handle it all like a champ and be our fearless little leader on days I felt the unsteady ground beneath me. We enjoyed the summer and then I remember it was maybe mid July and we went to the neighborhood pool and you made a friend. You swam with her and she shared her water Barbies with you and even told you about her YouTube channel and how many followers she had and I was thinking – wow – we are back in America. This didn't happen in Switzerland. Anyways, she left and we stayed for a little bit but you quickly became bored without your newfound companion and I wanted to go as well so we got in the car. I remember checking the rear view mirror to make sure you were in and I could start moving and I saw this look of sadness on your face and the start of some deep emotion welling up inside of you. It was like it hit you like a ton of bricks that you would be starting at a new school and didn't know anyone. That you didn't have ANY friends. I turned around to be there for you as you felt this emotion of being totally without your peeps. Of missing them. Of leaving behind a really good place and some really great friends. You felt sad, you expressed it, and you processed it pretty quickly. You didn't wallow in it – you expressed it, felt it, and moved forward with a look of possibility. I reminded you how quickly you made new friends and that we could see our families more often here and you could play with your cousins, etc., and then we drove by your "new" school so you could see the cool playground and start to try to feel familiar with it. As I held it together for you – I came home and cried. In flooded these feelings of – did we do the "right thing"? Did your daddy and I make the right decision? Would this move rock your boat for the rest of your life? I remember Stan's mom telling this story of how she moved from Germany to America around the age of five and people thought she was "different" and she got made fun of. This kind of haunted me for a sec. What if my precious Kirabelle was never the same. Then, I remembered everything I had learned again in my journey thus far. Your root is pretty solid. I was in a pretty amazing spot all throughout your pregnancy and through moving – we had gained confidence, grew tighter, and really got to know ourselves individually and as our small little family. So I pulled back out the voice of this will be okay – this is something you needed to feel and …well, I couldn't wait til school started.

Well, school started and within the first week I got contacted by your teacher because when it came to writing sentences – she thought you were behind. She said you would look sad and tell her you didn't know how. In my gut, I thought everything is new and you just need a little time. You had been at a bilingual school where it was German one week and English the next and maybe in your brain – there was some confusion on writing it in complete sentences coupled with everyone around you being brand new to you. It was hard with the teacher's somewhat tudey tone to not again question my decision but I knew Kira, I knew, you were capable. I knew your communication had been beyond your level since you were young. You spoke sentences at like two. I honestly just thought you needed to feel welcomed. You needed to feel at ease. You needed a bit of time to transition like Higgens before his teeth surgery. Like we all do – and that's okay! All I felt from her at first was pressure and a bit of freaking out.

Anyways a day later I got called that you had puked on the playground and I needed to come get you – oh boy – what a rough start. I quickly came and got you and we had had a pretty active past weekend so I figured you simply needed a bit of rest. So I kept you home the next day and we went and picked up a new puppy I had fallen in love with at this puppy boutique in New Jersey. WELCOME HOME MATILDA! Now I didn't plan on arriving home and adding anyone to the family but I was meeting my friend Stacy at Starbucks and happened to be early so I stopped in this boutique and I locked eyes with this cute little puppy to the upper left. I have never ever been so certain about something in my life (except maybe my first kiss with your daddy). But – like most major life decisions – I do like to consult your dad so I waited. We talked about it, I showed you pics, etc., and I was scheduled to go get her that day so even though you were home sick – you appeared better – so you came with me to get her. Matilda added so much joy and cuteness to our lives from day one. I didn't know anything about the breed – I honestly was simply touched by her soul. She was meant to be with us.

So as Matilda settled in, so did you and your teacher began to write emails telling me how great you were doing. Yes, mommy could breathe a big ole sigh of relief. So then I moved over to okay – what about my teaching journey.

Well – the road to find which studios to teach at and when – it wasn't without some bumps. The yoga scene here had totally transformed from what I remember. There were a good bit of different studios. The one I thought I was going to teach at because she had contacted me back in Switzerland and we had spoken – I wasn't sensing the right vibe and I was all about truly listening to my gut going forward and proceeding in the best way I could. So I let that relationship go and started teaching at my first yoga home, the community center, and online. I liked the vibe of the community center being different than a yoga studio. It created a different crowd and variety. I could see and learn about all bodies. I also started my own thing online hoping to build some private clients here in Pennsylvania. Well, this was quite another eye opening experience. Teaching online was a challenge. I remember the night before my FIRST CLASS and I couldn't get my camera to turn on and I was freaking out and took my computer to Best Buy only to learn that there is a switch on the right side of my PC that turns video OFF and I had accidentally hit it. Man. Lol. This is when I wished I had the support of an IT department like back at my finance gig. I was all ALONE. I was all ALONE in a SEA OF YOGA TEACHERS and who was I? Who was I to write this book? Man – this voice enters again. That inner disciplinary voice that sounds more like a critic and calls me a fraud sometimes is louder than that inner mentor voice that cheerleads me on and keeps me connected to my why. The two of them sometimes fight to get to the forefront. But as you know by now, mommy has had a good bit of practice in cultivating the mentor one to be the voice of reason, the one I want to turn to in hard times, the one that serves me well in life and helps me to live and love to the fullest. So I hope Kira – that you identify those voices within, their tone, where they are coming from. You aren't crazy. Don't let anyone tell you you are. You are human and we as humans are programmed to stay safe with a thirst to be free. Life is all about choices. Eliminate the right and wrong and the should do can do and connect with your innards, baby doll. Because I saw you before you were ever molded, touched, or programmed and it was a sight to behold. You are you. You are precious. You are already home.

After about a year of being home during the spring of your first year at the public school here – the pandemic hit. Prior to that I was a bit burned out from the move, from teaching, from pushing and driving forward so the idea of being "shut down" for two weeks with my family – had some upsides. Don't get me wrong the idea of a major pandemic wasn't cheery but I truly truly believe some of our best lessons come out of shitty times and shitty stuff and I was feeling a human disconnect way before the pandemic hit. To let go and have faith in that – and let it unfold – well that is tough. To remain present can be a challenge but I felt well versed in it. And thankful to be close to my family and not living so far from my family during this time.

So during the pandemic I took from my cancer tool belt what I had learned in times of crisis. Root down! I made sure I kept taking really good care of myself and of you. We continued with your bed time, good eating, not talking about it tons, time for faith and play, every Friday – we got take out. Take out Friday! It was something all of us looked forward to and enjoyed. And through this crisis – we cultivated some amazing memories and deeper bonds to family and close friends and community.

One particular memory I will share here is our anniversary celebration. Your daddy and I were celebrating our 12th wedding anniversary and despite not being able to go OUT to eat – we all dressed up anyways. We put on our best clothes and ordered Italian food and you made a schedule for the evening. We started with toasts. We each gave a toast and you used a white board with magnetic strawberry shortcake characters to depict Stan and I and our love story. It was super sweet. Then we danced. Daddy's dance moves in my opinion are enough to make anyone crack a smile even if their lips have been stuck in a frown position for years. I still can't figure out how someone can jerk their body quite in the way that he does. It is part of his charm. Then we ate, took some photos and got comfy to then play a game. Mommy won Jenga twice that night and I won't forget the joy in my heart that evening.

Speaking of relationships – marriage, Kira – my marriage to your daddy hasn't always been easy. We have both looked and battled with our own inner demons and at times it has drifted us far far apart. It's like you live with someone but you don't feel at all connected to them. There's a wall, a guard, an energetic force field between you two. What I can say is that looking back now – moving was amazing for us both as people and as a couple. Never stop working on yourself as an individual. Never stop carving out time for you because you will be a better person and a stronger member of a team, community, workplace, etc. The inner work has to be ongoing and continuous.

So what we learned in returning home was that there would also be people that seemed to hold this opinion that moving home was a step down or a loss or a failure and I sensed that and sat with it for a while. What is it about us humans that sometimes try to figure things out rather than accept that life can go in all sorts of freaking directions and the life route for some isn't the life for all?! This was another lesson in drowning out the noise, staying true to me, and proceeding forward. Was I crazy to leave such a beautiful Swiss life to come back to America? No. I was now filled with memories and a connection to both, and an experience that rooted me more deeply to myself.

The quote "home is where the heart is"...is a darn good one here, Kirabelle. I have felt home in that Baar Mcdonalds in Switzerland, in a chat with a friend, at a rest stop in Europe, at a lake in Zug, an ocean in Aruba, sitting on a couch cushion in my house, at church, in the presence of a nurse combing my hair back when I was sick. The list is endless and it can't be solved. It can only be felt in the heart. The stronger you cultivate your inner home and house clean from time to time, keep those windows sparkly, etc. – you will stay connected to you. And, well, you can always call your mamma as well!

Chapter Ten

GRIEF SUCKS

SO THINGS WERE CHURNING EVEN IN THE MIDST OF A PANDEMIC. THE complete shut down had been lifted and things were opening back up in the U.S. We all did have to wear a mask. We decided that summer to plan a trip to the Outer Banks with some of my college friends that I hadn't seen in quite some time. I was excited. I had been teaching (with the mask on) and online but the crowd had thinned, things were kind of depressing in the fitness/workout/yoga world. Nobody wanted to sweat with each other or touch each other and if they did come to class – peeps were pretty energetically frayed. Their flight or fight response had been activated by this entire ordeal and our cultural programming to push forward (myself included at times) was a bit extreme. So actually laughing, engaging, enjoying class wasn't like it had been before but as we moved through the pandemic – those real moments were being cultivated again. I felt proud that I was doing a good service to peeps and also to myself because again breathing and moving the body helps and I had been through crisis before and came out on the other side – stronger so I had high hopes for us all. In grief – the beauty in the fragility of life is brought to the forefront – I didn't know I was about to experience this grief again.

The Outer Banks was fun. I got a healthy dose of those positive ocean ions and some time with friends I had been deeply bonded to in college. There was one blow up at the end that I wish hadn't happened but I guess it does happen sometimes. What I did notice was that my period barely happened. There were only small amounts of blood. Energetically I felt great but it was weird and I figured I would watch it. I was hoping I wasn't going into menopause early but I was forty and there are side effects to chemo as I had mentioned.

Around September I joined this nutrition plan because I seemed to be gaining weight and couldn't figure out why as not much had changed. Maybe I was not eating quite as clean but I was definitely exercising and eating pretty good. The plan consisted of eating all good quality meat and eggs. I have touched on my eating disorder and bouts of bulimia in college and how yoga really allowed me more of an inside out approach but as my body ages and changes – body positivity is an ongoing healing process that guides me towards pure love and acceptance for ALL that I am. But again, seeing and feeling beauty in my innards takes less emphasis on my outers. Breaking the tie of self-worth to body size and of achieving a certain body size was a hard tie to break. It was a radical shift when I felt love and light inside and didn't give two shits what my physical appearance was doing. This felt godly and this was my jam now but I sometimes slipped back. So in teaching yoga – I put even MORE pressure on myself that to be a good teacher and to sell myself – I had to look a certain way with a certain amount of muscle mass and a certain healthy skin tone. Man – the pressure was enough to drive me bonkers and/or sometimes want to quit. How could I go down this path again? How could I have not learned from my previous teacher Mrs. Cancer that this shiz doesn't matter. Well, I am human. And a vulnerable lovely one. So I started the program and at the end of the six weeks I had only lost a pound or two and still wasn't having a legit period so I went to the doc.

He tested my hormones and one was out of whack so he wanted me to get my pituitary checked out with an MRI which I scheduled.

Before this appointment – on a Friday – I felt really weird that day. I thought maybe it was hormones or something. I remember barely getting through my 1:00 P.M. class. It was awful. After class I took myself to my favorite green juice/smoothie/coffee shop to reward myself and hoping to lift this shitty feeling by getting a drink and whilst I was there – the owner sent me home with these free almond milks he wanted me to try. I love the couple that owns this place. They are so amazing and have the most awesome story and passion for sharing healthy eats and nutrients to the body. I smiled and accepted them but something still didn't feel right so I went home and laid down.

Around 4 P.M. – intense pain came. I mean it was undeniable that something in my uterus/bladder/vagina area was not right. I tried to wait until five because Stan was working from the home office as per usual during covid but I think at about 4:40 I broke in and said I need to go to the ER – something is wrong. In my mind – I tried to rationalize that maybe just maybe it was a really bad UTI. The "omg what if it's cancer again" was only a small blip on the way back screen ...it was just a lot of breathing and a lot of let go, let God. We got there, checked in and waited. It felt better to stand than to sit and I noticed the pain would come and go, wax and wane.

Finally, they took me back and got some pain meds administered, I had peed in a cup, etc. I remember one nurse this time really complaining to me about her mask and how her mask was causing her breakouts and I was like – I am sorry but I can't listen right now – I am in pain. And she stopped.

Then a doc came in to update me and said the urine sample was fine – they were going to do an X-ray or image of my belly to see if there was a kidney stone. I remember thinking to myself – how but okay – pass it and I can move on. Then I started wondering how this could happen – I don't drink that much tea?

It was getting to be late and we were not sure how long I was going to be there so we called our neighbor (another angelic godsend since my return back home) to see if Stan could bring you to her house for the night or until we got home later and she said sure of course.

Then another doctor came in – I remember his face clearly – because in that moment he told me the imaging didn't reveal any kidney stone – that they saw a baby. That I was pregnant. In that moment – and I kid you not – it was like this light came from above in the upper left corner of the room and it just sent a lot of love and peace my way. It was like it was telling me – you are meant to be a mom. You are a wonderful mom and you are enough. You haven't failed anyone. It was kind of like "are you there Becky" …it's me again! Life's best teacher – enter another pivotal moment of which I lost control of all my emotions …. I had surrendered and was now leaning on a room full of amazing strangers and a sea of unknown ahead.

It was this awakening that I didn't need to prove anything, that I wasn't a failure – that I was an excellent mom. And I filled up with such love, such hope at the thought of a new little baby. I also had a bit of regret for pushing so hard and not knowing sooner. Sometimes in life it is great to search and seek and to want to be better and do better and achieve your goals – but I had become a bit disconnected from also spending time in real moments completely okay with life as it is. In the lens of gratitude for what I had.

So I smiled and jokingly said that can't be – my husband and I have been so "busy" recently we hadn't had much sex and he kinda joked and said the one-liner "well, they say it only takes one time" and we both shared a real moment – a laugh. And then I was thinking to myself – shit is this like a divine intervention or Blessed Mary moment but she doesn't curse and I am not fucking her..... I also kind of felt highly embarrassed because I used to watch Maury Povich all the time and this shiz was perfect for that show but how could I not know I was preggers? This is where blame and shame could have entered but radical compassion for myself and my humanness took place.

Then I called Stan and told him and your daddy has always wanted another baby. I am the one who doubted that I could be as healthy as I was when I had you and that I could give as much love as when I had you and still not lose me and my dreams. I didn't think I could ever do or have it all. I also didn't feel completely supported emotionally in the way I felt I needed to be to embark on this adventure again but your daddy and I had done a ton of work and self-growth and I was open to it again. In one quick call – I told him they had found a baby and he was on his way back to the hospital from dropping you at our neighbors Carrie's so I couldn't wait to see him when he got back. A baby was much more amazing news than a kidney stone.

As I laid on the bed – I also heard someone in the hall lose a loved one. She was crying uncontrollably shouting, "We lost him, we lost him – I need to find (so and so)." I couldn't hear all of what she said – but it was apparent someone she loved had left this world. I wondered if it was covid, if they were sick – I wondered what the details were but the pain was heard clear as day.

As another lady came in to give me an ultrasound – she was very quiet and the pain I was having in the nether regions continued and because it was spaced out – it seemed to be somewhat like contractions. So my gut instinct wasn't that this was good news and your daddy felt it as well. There was no heartbeat. So in the course of about three hours we went from pure hope to pure sadness. To have loved and lost in that moment. To have hope and feel shattered. It felt like this rug was swept out from underneath me and I went from the highest high to the lowest low. Jimmy V would say this was a full day. In that moment, it felt like my worst. My hand was lovingly on my belly, on that baby from the second I found out she was there until she was removed from me. And what I have learned about grief or big life shit as I'll call it – you can grieve it and think you are done – but it is a process – one of which you won't have complete control over. I am crying now as I type this. It is still raw and real at times.

I had some really amazing docs that night. I remember Nurse Muriel and Nurse Monica (Monica is my sister's name) and they held my hand, felt my sadness, and told my husband that this would hit me hard and to watch me. They channeled love into me at a time I needed to know I wasn't alone. I needed to see the beauty of human love during loss…even amongst strangers. I saw it. I felt it. I am grateful for it.

We said goodbye to your little sis that night. She is our little angel. Our connector to Heaven and Earth. And as tough as that experience was – there were real moments and real beauty in life felt that night.

We came home and I was happy to be home, to be out of pain, to go to sleep. I slept until around eight or nine the next day which is not typical for me and then woke up and vomited everything I think I had been given the night before. I did feel better afterwards. Then I told my neighbor what had actually happened because the kidney stone didn't feel like how I wanted to leave it and she was amazingly incredible. She listened. She brought over some hand-picked flowers later and she checked on me. She also told me she had a friend I could talk to who had a miscarriage if I wanted to speak to someone who could relate.

I took a week off of teaching to "grieve" and told myself to feel it, cry, take walks, be with nature and all of those healing things I knew would be good for me. I also wrote her this poem. You have heard it and I am going to leave it here because – this was my message for her…

Miscarriage is one of those things that I feel like the cage put on it is to not announce it or name the child or tell too many people because it was not a full term pregnancy. And well – I don't like cages. I don't like this cage. She was real. She was a life that was lost. She is forever a part of our family that we told you about and we will talk about her whenever she comes up. We will honor her. She was my beautiful "Dance with Pink".

~~~

Dance With Pink
You were my dance with Pink
And it was the most precious dance
It didn't last very long
And I never saw your face
I never touched your hands or feet
Our souls danced together and you brought pieces of me back to life
You breathed life into me and me into you and for a while we were one
And then you were gone
So short, so quick, it was like a dream
You were with me and then you weren't
You were in my house and then you left
My womb is empty but my heart is forever engraved
with your unknown initials
Your spirit that I danced with had such familiarity
Yet there was not enough time to love you, to know you, to see you
I know you'll come again from time to time in the form
of a sunset or a breeze
And we will dance again
But you weren't meant to stay, you were called by God

To do work at a different angle, different vantage point
I want you to know
That I love you…
And I am forever changed by
That precious dance of pink
—-Mom

So even though my mind wanted to give myself a week and thought I could spend time in nature, cry, and fast and all the negative sadness would leave my body….this was not the case. My oftentimes wiser heart knows that again, it's an ongoing process of which I have to surrender to at sometimes the most inopportune times. Healing isn't something I can put a time stamp on. I needed to allow myself space to feel and when it arose – let it arise and be vulnerable with the peeps I trusted with my heart.

So grief – well – it does sting. It does suck. It's heavy. It can take your breath away. It can make your heart and chest feel like it's going to explode. It can make you want to build walls around your heart like walls some peeps wanna build around the US. I still think cultivating practices that help you to be with yourself while you feel it is an amazing gift that you can give yourself.

Grief is also as we go through life unavoidable and part of what makes the time we do have on this earth – so darn beautiful. So with all of the deaths of COVID – it makes sense that we are experiencing some collective grief, tiredness, anxiety, sadness, maybe a questioning of where do we go from here? It is human.

Chapter Eleven

LOVE HEALS...AGAIN

LOVE IS, I BELIEVE, THE MOST POWERFUL POTION OUT THERE. I KNOW sometimes to some it sounds so very simple to love but honestly my journey of self-love has been an ongoing daily practice – just like my time on the mat. And I tell you this because I wish differently for you. I wish for you to always see yourself as a beautifully made human and on the days that you don't – that your inner voice be one that speaks to you with love and encourages you to still try to put yourself out there and to be honest if you want or need a little encouragement. Being vulnerable is not weak. Being nice is not fake. Everything has labels but when we remove the labels – we connect at our deepest cores and at our deepest cores – there is a lot of love and light.

I often wish at times we promoted this medicine more than the ones that come in white pills or cortisol shots because it is powerful.

The people that were kind and accepting of me during my darkest times – they lifted me and carried me along my journey. They gave me real moments of pure human exchange, hope in humanity, and a want to make it through. I may never totally be over the loss of your sis. It still evokes tears and sometimes I wish desperately to have met her. But I also feel completely blessed for the love I received during my pregnancy with her and for the connection to heaven that you, your daddy, and I have. She is our little navigator up there. Popping in on us from time to time and loving us from afar. And the fact that maybe she is hanging out with my grandmother – the lady who was one of my most amazing female mentors – that is pretty cool.

So as I went back to teach – I was a bit nervous – because I wasn't sure if anyone knew, if I should tell them, or if I would just carry on as if nothing happened which never feels totally right. Your daddy has his programming and I have mine. And again – neither one is right or wrong. He tends to keep things close to his chest and didn't really want to tell too many people and it was the same with my illness. I, on the other hand, needed to share, needed to cry, was okay reaching for support. And what we are much better at now is allowing each other the space and grace to do what we need, so that we can come back together more whole. We are simply different and our work within is different and that is totally okay. Where it gets divisive is if we try to control the other. When I would start to wonder if I should be more like him or if I was being weak – I was creating a divide within me that was diminishing my inner strengths. Sometimes – we are our own creator of cracks in our foundation. Thankfully – I have my faith and my yoga practice that have both taught me a lot about staying with me, listening to my inner mentor, honoring my strengths, honoring both the masculine and feminine within, while also working on my weaknesses and being fully present especially when stuff gets tough.

I remember teaching my silver sneakers class that Friday and one of the ladies was a bit upset that there wasn't more advanced warning about class being cancelled the Friday before and so I did tell her in front of some other ladies and right away her what appeared somewhat sternness about showing up and there being no class…transformed into

– "I am so sorry." Energetically she shifted. She stepped out of her world and into mine and we simply moved past it. I was able to stay present and teach a great class and in sharing something tough – I think it actually bonded us more. Sometimes I look at teachers or certain people as always having it all figured out and the truth is – none of us do. As Nightbirde so beautifully sings sometimes – we are all a little lost and that is OKAY. Keep showing up. Keep being you.

Now the first period after my miscarriage – woah – I wish someone had told me it would be like my hormones bottoming out. Weirdly it felt like any last piece of her was rushing out of my body with a crud ton of blood. Tears were shed and I felt such low lows that I had no idea that there was any bouncing back. But – life – when it takes you down – there truly is no place to go but up again….and then back down and then up and in circles ……again the beauty of it. You will never have it figured out and when you try to control – you actually do a disservice to yourself. I can kind of relate this breakdown to when I thought life was over as my tongue swelled. The moment I let go into what I was feeling and went there and reminded myself I was not alone – life rushed in again. Something larger than myself was out there. I was never alone. You are not either.

The gyno called me the following week and I told them and she was like "why didn't you call us!?" in a very loving manner and I was like well – I am fine now – it passed. But I could hear in her voice the acknowledgement of the magnitude of losing a baby even if the baby was never born alive or seen or could have had problems. It is a loss. A really mother fucking sad one (yes – mommy did curse there and sometimes that's okay too Kira). And love – love of friends, families and strangers – can help move you through it. It's like that footprints in the sand book mark I had when I was young, – there are times in life I carried others and times in life I had to be carried. There are times I sent ripples out into this world and times those ripples engulfed me so much that I was moved.

With each day and each period – I got back into the swing of life. It helped that from time to time you would bring her up in a way to include her and you had your own process of grieving and of feeling all the feels and I encouraged you to not hold back with those. And I have to tell you, you taught me resilience. You taught me about letting go. It was so clear to me that when daddy and I told you – that you clearly moved through all the stages. First you were shocked. Because when you left the hospital you thought I had a kidney stone. Then you were sad. Deeply sad. And then you moved into speaking about her, honoring her, and hoping for the future. To hear your perspective, to be there to feel your feels – I am forever grateful for you, Kirabelle.

That November after the miscarriage, we went to Aruba and it was a very healing bonding trip. Stan's dad was supposed to come but he had an infection so it was Stan's mom, me, you, and Daddy. Stan's mom – your Oma – had also lost a baby so she knew the pain and weirdly, your sis may have been the one to help our relationship move forward. I remember we were in the back of the rental car and we had just come from a beautiful beach and did some snorkeling and you got your little notepad out and started drawing our family. And you included her. And you showed Oma so proud that that was your sister. I welled up with tears in the front but I can't label them as sad tears because that wasn't the exact emotion I was feeling– I can only label them as tears of love. The kind of love that touches you so deep within – that you feel so connected to life and earth and God. And Love....it Heals.

Chapter Twelve

ONWARD ALWAYS

WE GOT BACK FROM VACATION AND I FELT IN A PRETTY GOOD SPOT overall. Aruba really is one happy island. Despite covid being a thing – the ocean, the salt water, the sun, the sand were all refreshing to my body, mind, and soul.

Oh whilst we were there in Aruba– we embarked on the most incredible adventure. We let ourselves out of the cage. Together. So your daddy is afraid of heights and it is about the only thing that I am less afraid of than him probably. I am also guaranteed to beat him at Scrabble. He's a water baby and you love it too but honestly deep water has always brought up some deep stuff in mommy. Except the time in Bora Bora with the merman.

Anyways, back to Aruba – so I have always wanted to go parasailing and we finally did it. We got on the boat and I felt in good hands. But once we got harnessed in (or is it called buckled?!) ....and I saw that our legs are actually dangling and you would be dangling next to me – I freaked out a bit. I was logically trying to figure out how we go up and how we get down and how we don't land in the water, etc., etc. I think your daddy was figuring out where to put his boy parts so that he didn't have a parasailing injury and felt comfy cozy up there. My brain took over and I white knuckled the first five minutes or so of the ride. But I was able to remind myself of what faithful adventures we had embarked on so far – and what all we have learned in the process. I have grown so much and healed so much and I am so proud of that. So never let anyone tell you that what you are in your twenties is set for life or any other age or that once you reach a certain age the rest is downhill. I really believe life is a unique beautiful journey for all of us and no one knows the end to your story. No one holds the pen but you and God. I recently was part of a yoga teacher summit and this lady described viewing life like a play with the first act, second act, and third etc. I liked that better than thinking of it as this bell curve of you go up and then you go down and die.

While up in the air, it felt amazing to look back on my life at a bird's view and see all that not just I had overcome and grown through but how connected we were as a little family of three, plus an angel (plus two pups at home). It was amazing to look over and see your joy that was so much larger than your fear. You felt safe in the air. You felt safe with us. You felt safe with these two "strangers" guiding us on this adventure in this land far from home. Life is scary sometimes so it is easy to become caged and make your cage super ducking cozy– but it's so freakin' amazing to let yourself out of the cage, to surrender, to breathe in fresh air and to change your vantage point. Now this can be achieved in MANY ways other than parasailing but for today – this was where it was at. We were soaring thousands of feet above a land crippled by covid right now. We smiled a lot and laughed together up there and on the descent – I talked to God. I thanked God for everything, for this experience of being alive, of having you and your dad in my life, of being able to do things like this, for those affected by covid, and I sent a big hug to your sis.

We returned from Aruba and got ready for the holiday season which I am pretty ducking positive I have already stated is my favorite time of year. Yes, Mommy repeats herself. So does daddy. If you are really listening – you will get to know another human being really well because they will repeat themselves sometimes, they will give you little clues to their inner state, and if they do the same in return – you both will be able to love and nourish each other better.

Christmas was also full of emotion because it was supposed to be my entire family, but on the week before my sister and brother and their families cancelled due to covid and being afraid of exposing my parents. So – that was sad. My mom enjoys having ALL of us and I can't imagine what it would mean to me to get to that age and see my children and my children's children at the holidays. Now God works in mysterious ways so that Christmas while it wasn't what was envisioned – it was special. When else would we come to Virginia and not also see my bro, sis and families? I love this memory and especially loved seeing my mom open her Ruth Bader Ginsberg ornament.

The February after Christmas – I finished my teacher training and became a 500 hour certified yoga teacher, through Brett Larkin's Uplifted Program. About a year ago I thought I was going to Bali to do this but instead I did it online. And I have to say whilst I had reservations about online being the same or getting as much out of it – it was an incredibly amazing experience. I learned so much and was really able to see how even in teaching – I put a lot of pressure on myself and it took me out of the present. I had this idea that if I got more training – then I would "be ready". Ready to what? Ready to teach? Ready to go off a high dive? I was already ready. At my core – I was already okay. I just needed to believe it, to keep doing it, and to keep on keeping on. I saw so much of myself in some of the other teachers. We all had unique stories, journeys, perspectives and ways of teaching and no two paths were the same but there were some blocks in all of us and a desire to work through those, form community, and continue to learn. Some people owned studios, for some it was a side gig, etc. It was a very diverse group.

After graduation – I continued teaching and another bump came. One of the studios I taught at was closing and this opened up my Monday/Friday schedule and at first I was frantic to fill it and then as I sat back – I remembered this book. This thing I wanted to complete for so long that felt some days like I could touch it and others like it was so far away and so very unattainable. It was a thought, a seed, that arrived with the birth of you and then I didn't nourish it so for a while it became dark again. AND THAT IS OKAY. Because it needed time. I needed time. I needed to find my groove into motherhood. I need to release judgement of how long it was going to take. I needed to be patient. I needed to live.

Chapter Thirteen

I SURRENDER

ALL SIGNALS WERE POINTING TO THE FACT THAT I WAS LEARNING AGAIN to have more grace with myself. I needed to use some of what I learned to release control of outcomes so that I could regain control of my real moments and happiness. You will understand this as you go through life and work towards goals that sometimes there is a PUSH involved to finish. And that push is fine but must be balanced with some pull. I was pushing. Your daddy can be a pusher. I think crisis (aka covid) brings out a lot of deep push programming. We see it in our physical bodies. Depression is up, my dentist told me the other day that teeth grinding is up 40 percent during covid, even deodorant sales are sky rocketing.

I think the best thing to do during crisis is to both root down but also allow for that release to a higher power – whatever that power or school of thought you believe in where you alone don't hold all the answers and you cannot keep yourself from dying. You can protect yourself. You can continue to be a good person and grow and take care of those around you. But you don't hold the ONE solution to this crisis. If you surrender and look back at it – I think you can see more of a different healing journey to be obtained by each of us from this pandemic.

Whenever I surrender on my mat after a really good yoga class or a really hard day – I find such peace in surrender. I lay my tired weary physical body on that mat and I just drop beneath and feel the flow of life inside. I turn my focus from the external to my breath. I simplify things for a moment and take awe of the beauty and expansiveness of each inhale and the release and flow obtained in the complete exhale. And then when I come to move again – I am moving from a place of balance and center that feels oh so good. And by coming home again and again and again to myself – it's like I chose me just as I chose my partner again and again and again and it is what keeps relationships in the green in my book.

Now the practice of surrender doesn't have to be only on the mat. I have taken it off the mat into many different areas. I love prayer and music and cooking without a recipe and trying out new spots and breaking routine. I have taken it into teaching. The classes that I feel I teach the best are when I surrender to the unknown. When I let go and my biggest intention is to stay present with myself and the students and if I feel the need for a shift – honor that voice. And with parenting – oh nelly – there are times I want to protect you from so much. But deep down I know that I can't. I know that I can provide you a safe sturdy foundation and I feel as though I have but the rest – you have to live and experience and fail and flourish and fall and make mistakes and say things you don't mean and eat too many chocolates and do all the things. I want you to experience ALL of the things. I want you to ask yourself the tough questions when you need to and to be you and at this stage you are so darn good at that. So just know that there will be times of crisis and in them – leave room for surrender and grace both for yourself and those around you. There is wisdom to be found here but it can't be found always pushing forward. Or turning to blame and shame.

The Final Chapter
(Kind of like the final countdown...)
THE REST IS STILL UNWRITTEN

SO I ORIGINALLY HAD HIGH HOPES, KIRA, OF THIS BOOK ENDING WITH me having achieved all of my dreams – maybe another baby or an uber successful online teaching business and I decided to end it with not a major accomplishment but an inward love for the person I have become and the exact place I am in. I honestly don't know what the future holds but what I do know is – that I am so alive and so here and so thankful for you, this writing journey, and these real moments.

And my hope for this book is to remind you that true peace and contentment – there are within you and that they do have an impact on all other things in your life. Never stop returning to you. Never stop dropping inside of the physical body and mental space to feel the core of who you are and to connect with that which is divine. Never stop working on you. Dream Big. Work Hard. Love with all of your heart even when you may feel like the world tells you to stop. Let yourself out of the cage periodically to check in on how caged you have become. Love your body. Move your body. From fingers to toes and everything in between. Get to know your body on a deep level. Deep. Accept that your body may change and you may have little to no control over how to "fix" it because it doesn't need to be fixed – it needs to be loved and accepted. It is the house to your soul and no matter what kind of paint you use on the outside – don't abandon the innards. Speak. Use your voice. Learn to use your voice again and again. Play with your voice. Sing Loud. Do karaoke. Chant. Stick your tongue out. Dance. Dance in the rain and the cold and with the sun beaming down on your face. Be aware. Aware of how you feel, how others feel around you. Be grateful. Grateful for the life you were given and aware that your journey is different than others. Create. Create experiences, things, food, relationships, paintings, whatever your heart calls you to create. Never stop learning. Learning creates connections inside and out. It sparks light, life and inspiration. Work towards the highest good of all in all that you do. Trust. Trust yourself and others until they give you a reason not to and then forgive. Forgive fully. Not just a little. If someone does break your trust again – have boundaries but also have faith that they can change too. That anything can be overcome. That light does drive out dark. That Love. Love always prevails.

And please know Kirabelle – that whether I am in your life here on earth or a star up in heaven – I am your biggest supporter, cheerleader, believer, motivator, and encourager, and I have also been…your student as you have been mine.

Love Always,
Mom